Poverty, Inequality and
Income Distribution in
Comparative Perspective

Poverty, Inequality and Income Distribution in Comparative Perspective

The Luxembourg Income Study (LIS)

edited by

Timothy M. Smeeding
Michael O'Higgins
Lee Rainwater

with an introduction by

A. B. Atkinson

 HARVESTER
WHEATSHEAF

New York   London   Toronto   Sydney   Tokyo   Singapore

First published 1990 by
Harvester Wheatsheaf
66 Wood Lane End, Hemel Hempstead
Hertfordshire HP2 4RG
A division of
Simon & Schuster International Group

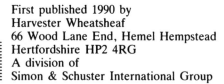

Typeset in 10/12 pt Times
by Photo·graphics, Honiton, Devon

Printed and bound in Great Britain by
Billing and Sons Limited, Worcester

British Library Cataloguing-in-Publication Data

Poverty, inequality and income distribution in comparative
  perspective.
  1. Income. Distribution. Measurement
  I. Smeeding, Timothy, *1948–* II. O'Higgins, Michael,
  1954– III. Rainwater, Lee
  339.2

  ISBN 0–7450–0335–4

---

1 2 3 4 5   94 93 92 91 90

For Ryan, Erin and Carol

who gave us the time to build LIS

CONTENTS

Contributors   ix

Foreword   xiii
  Lee Rainwater and Gaston Schaber

Introduction   xv
  A.B. Atkinson

**1 The LIS Database: Technical and Methodological
  Aspects**   1
  Timothy M. Smeeding and Günther Schmaus

**2 Income Distribution and Redistribution: A Microdata
  Analysis for Seven Countries**   20
  *Michael O'Higgins, Günther Schmaus and Geoffrey
  Stephenson*

**3 Income Poverty in Seven Countries: Initial Estimates
  from the LIS Database**   57
  *Timothy M. Smeeding, Lee Rainwater, Martin Rein,
  Richard Hauser and Gaston Schaber*

4 Age and Income in Contemporary Society   77
  Peter Hedstrom and Stein Ringen

5 Retirement and Well-being Among the Elderly   105
Lea Achdut and Yossi Tamir

6 Economic Well-being Among One-parent Families   126
Richard Hauser and Ingo Fischer

**7 The Significance of LIS for Comparative Social Policy
Research**   158
*Michael O'Higgins, Lee Rainwater and Timothy
M. Smeeding*

Appendix
A User's Guide to the LIS Database   172

Bibliography   182

Index   186

CONTRIBUTORS

Lea Achdut is the head of the Basic Research Department in the Bureau of Research and Planning, National Insurance Institute, Jerusalem, Israel. Her previous research concerns income inequality and poverty in Israel, and the economics of old age. Recent publications include 'The Anatomy of Changes in Poverty and Income Inequality Under Rapid Inflation: Israel: 1979–1984.'

A.B. Atkinson is Tooke Professor of Economic Science and Statistics at the London School of Economics. He has written on the distribution of income and wealth, and on public economics with particular reference to taxation and social security. He is currently President of the European Economic Association and was President of the Econometric Society in 1988.

Ingo Fischer born in 1958, is research associate at the Special Collaborative Programme 3 'Microanalytical Foundations of Social Policy' as well as teaching assistant in the Department of Economics at the University of Frankfurt. As LIS country coordinator for West Germany he participated in preparing the West German data file. His areas of interest are international comparisons of social security systems, poverty problems and income distribution.

Richard Hauser is Professor of Social Policy at the University of Frankfurt and director of a research project on 'Social Policy and Income Distribution' which is part of the Special Collaborative Programme 3 at the Universities of Frankfurt and Mannheim. During 1986/88 he was Vicepresident of the University of Frankfurt. He was adviser to the German Chancellery, various

Ministries and the Commission of the European Community. His areas of interest are economic and social policy, distribution of income and wealth, international comparisons of social security systems.

Peter Hedstrom is an Assistant Professor of Sociology at the University of Chicago. His current research focuses on earnings inequalities and promotion processes within work organisations. He serves as Associate Editor for both the *American Journal of Sociology* and *Rationality and Society*.

Michael O'Higgins is a managing consultant with Price Waterhouse, London, seconded to the Social Affairs Division of the OECD, Paris, during 1987/88. He is also a member of the Society and Politics Research Development Group of the UK Economic and Social Research Council and a specialist adviser to the House of Commons Select Committee on Social Services. Much of his work on LIS was carried out while he was a Reader in Social Policy at the University of Bath, UK, and during periods as a Visiting Scholar in the Department of Sociology, Harvard University, and as a Visiting Fellow in the Social Justice Project at the Australian National University, Canberra. Neither current nor past employers or hosts bear any responsibility for any views expressed here.

Lee Rainwater is research director of the Luxembourg Income Study and Professor of Sociology at Harvard University. His research work for the past several years has been concerned with comparative studies of social and economic well-being. He is co-author of *Income Packaging in the Welfare State*.

Martin Rein is Professor of Social Policy at the Massachusetts Institute of Technology in the Department of Urban Studies and Planning. He is co-author of *Income Packaging in the Welfare State* and *Stagnation and Renewal in the Welfare State*.

Stein Ringen was (acting) Professor of Welfare Studies at the University of Stockholm whilst working on LIS. He is currently an assistant director general in the Norwegian Ministry of Justice.

Gaston Schaber is Director of the Centre d'Etudes de Population, de Pauvreté et de Politiques Socioéconomiques (CEPS), Luxembourg, and a principal counsellor to the Prime Minister of Luxembourg. He holds faculty appointments at the University of Liège, Belgium, and at Clark University, Worcester, MA, USA.

Günther Schmaus is a senior consultant of Computer Resources International (CRI) in Copenhagen. Since 1985 he has worked for the Centre d'Etudes de Population, de Pauvreté et de Politiques Socioéconomiques (CEPS/INSTEAD), Luxembourg. Now he is working as a software consultant for the Luxembourg Panel Study (PSELL) of CEPS/INSTEAD and is involved in coordinating the process of improving software infrastructure and analysis of Panel data.

Timothy Smeeding is overall project director of the Luxembourg Income Study, Professor of Public Policy and Economics, Vanderbilt University, and Director of the Center for the Study of Families, Children, and the Elderly, Vanderbilt Institute for Public Policy Studies. His research interests are in the economics of social welfare policy, cross-national comparisons of economic well-being and poverty, and the economics of children and aged. Recent publications include *The Vulnerable* and 'Poor Children in Rich Countries.'

Geoffrey Stephenson is a principal consultant with Logica SA, Luxembourg.

Yossi Tamir is senior researcher in the Bureau of Research and Planning, National Insurance Institute, Jerusalem, Israel. His research interests include comparative studies of retirement and ageing and income inequality in Israel.

FOREWORD

Lee Rainwater and Gaston Schaber

Comparative explorations of the distribution of economic well-being have been a long-running interest of social scientists. With the rise of welfare state expenditures this theoretical interest has been reinforced by policy interest in who benefits, and by how much, from the massive redistribution of income involved in social security and other income maintenance programmes. But precise and systematic comparative explorations of these issues have been hampered by the unavailability of comparative data.

For a decade or longer policy analysts in many nations have been able to describe with increasing precision the distribution of income, and the effect on that distribution of the wage-setting and transfer institutions of their societies. It remained to bring together these similar enterprises to make possible truly scientific comparative work on the distribution and redistribution of economic well-being. This book reports the first results of this effort. So far as we are aware, the Luxembourg Income Study (LIS) data utility is the first academically managed comparative microdata resource to be constructed to facilitate the work of comparative scholars. We believe that databanks such as LIS, which assemble comparable microdata from several countries, will prove increasingly valuable to social science and policy research in the future.

Our effort is a result of a meeting between European and American policy researchers at Clark University in the summer of 1982. The conference was devoted to an assessment of the current state of knowledge and methodology in the study of low income. Most of the Americans involved had little exposure to discussions of these issues in other countries. Because many of the Europeans had recently been involved in studying poverty problems in the whole of the European Community, the issue of comparison quickly came to the fore. The group determined that the time was ripe for an effort to construct a cross-national dataset. The technology of income surveys was sufficiently similar from country to country to allow this. The goal was not a comparative study but rather the creation of a comparative research data utility which would be useful to a wide range of academic and policy researchers.

This effort posed daunting political as well as technical problems. In some of the countries to be represented income surveys were freely available to researchers. The willingness of the Luxembourg Government, with the personal involvement of Prime Minister Jacques Santer, to provide a home for the project, as well as providing the initial funding, proved crucial in bringing together in one place data from countries with such diverse policies on data availability. Our thanks must also go to Geoffrey Stephenson who provided LIS with the expert assistance of Günther Schmaus through CRI enterprises. Without their technical expertise the data on which these initial papers are based would not be possible.

Given that data collection is enormously expensive, and that analysis can serve diverse purposes, it is obviously highly efficient to make social and economic surveys widely available. It is nonetheless a challenge to governments and scholars to work out ways of ensuring such wide availability while minimising risks to respondents, and to the integrity of national statistical enterprises.

Without the continuing support and assistance of the Luxembourg Government Computing Centre (C.I.E.) the LIS project would not be possible. We thank its director, Mr Felix Schumacher, and the Centre's staff, in particular Mr Claude Conzemius, for their energetic efforts for LIS.

We offer these initial analyses of the LIS data as examples of the kind of knowledge that can be developed from a carefully designed comparative databank. Much more can and will be done with LIS. (We describe how the data can be used in the Appendix to this book.) Extension of the LIS concept to comparative longitudinal studies, and to comparative labour force surveys is feasible today; in fact the search for comparability in these complex matters is a major goal of the LIS home, the Centre for Population, Poverty and Policy Studies, in Luxembourg. As understanding of how such databases can be planned and constructed spreads in the social sciences, we can expect a rich harvest of knowledge to follow from overcoming the boundaries of nations in our analyses of society and economy.

INTRODUCTION

A.B. Atkinson

THE LIS PROJECT

The Luxembourg Income Study (LIS) is, in my view, one of the most exciting developments in applied economic research of recent years. The use of household surveys for the study of poverty and income inequality has grown greatly, with the increasing availability to academic researchers of the individual microdata. In the United Kingdom, for example, the Family Expenditure Survey has provided a rich source of information. In the United States, there have been many studies using the Current Population Survey, which provides, among other things, the basis for the official poverty count. What has not been possible – until the advent of LIS – is access to microdata sets for a wide range of different countries on a comparable basis. This new database makes it possible to address questions such as the following. How does poverty in the United States differ in scale and composition from that in other countries? How do the elderly fare in different OECD (Organisation for Economic Cooperation and Development) countries? How do differences, across countries, in economic circumstances and social policies affect the relative position of single-parent families?

In order to answer these questions, one could of course put the study by Professor X for one country alongside that by Professor Y for another country. However, anyone who has tried this exercise will know that such a comparison of results typically brings to light major differences in approach and methods. Professor X took the household as the unit of analysis; Professor Y took the nuclear family. Professor X took total income without any adjustment for family size; Professor Y took income per equivalent adult using his patent equivalence scale. The finding that poverty was higher in one country than another may then be due as much to differences in the measuring rod as to genuine differences in circumstances. It may be possible to adjust for some of the differences by using the tables publishcd in the separate national sources, but this is usually a frustrating business. What one needs, in order to eliminate the differences in method, and to minimise the differences due to the form in which the information has been collected, is access to the original data. With the surveys for different countries side by side, it is possible to apply the same equivalence scales or to take more closely comparable units of analysis.

The great achievement of the LIS project is to have brought together microdata sets for a wide range of different countries and to have made them accessible for this kind of research. I must confess that, when I first heard of the plan, I was sceptical as to its feasibility. As a prospective research investment, it seemed to belong in the high risk category: if it had not come off, a lot of resources would have led to very little output. As Lee Rainwater and Gaston Schaber point out in their Foreword, there were daunting political problems in addition to the sheer technical complexity. Access to data is an extremely sensitive issue. International comparisons often supply political ammunition, as was illustrated by *Le Monde*'s award of *La Médaille d'Or* to France on the basis of an OECD comparison of income inequality which showed that country on top (Sawyer, 1976).

By the time of the first Conference in Luxembourg – held in the hospitable Centre for Population, Poverty and Policy Studies – at which the papers in this volume were first presented, I had been converted. By then the LIS dataset covered seven countries – Canada, Israel, Norway, Sweden, the United Kingdom, the United States and West Germany – and more were on their way. The results from the papers confirmed that the data would indeed allow work on cross-country comparisons of income distribution to be raised to a new level.

Of course, not all the problems of comparability can be overcome. The LIS project is constrained by the form in which the data are collected and made available in each of the countries. If the survey for one country did not collect annual income data, then there is no way in which its absence can be completely rectified. If the second family in a multi-family household is not separately identified, as in the Israeli and West German surveys (see Chapter 1), then the information cannot be resurrected. What the project *can* do is to offer the user different options. The user can choose whether to concentrate on countries with the same definitions or whether to make adjustments to the individual data; and in the latter case there may be a choice of methods.

It is for this reason that *access* to the data is a crucial feature of the LIS project. In this way, the LIS team are supplying a public good to the research community. The seriousness with which this role is taken is well illustrated by the Summer Workshop Series, launched in 1988, at which some 25 doctoral and post-doctoral students spend two weeks learning about the LIS database and developing research projects making use of the data.

At the same time, this emphasis on access has been costly for the LIS project. It has undoubtedly added to the complexity of the negotiations with the government departments responsible for the original data. The documentation required (a flavour of which is provided by the Appendix) is of a quite different order when intended for a potential audience of outsiders. The flow of enquiries from around the world must at times test the patience of the LIS technical team. This in turn raises the question of the funding of such a public service, a challenge which has been taken up by funding agencies in the majority of LIS countries, in addition to the generous core support provided by the Government of Luxembourg and by Computer Resources Incorporated. Social science researchers must be grateful that they have responded to this imaginative project in an imaginative way.

That this has been possible is a tribute to the intellectual drive and missionary enthusiasm of the LIS Project Director, Tim Smeeding, to the support of his co-editors, Michael O'Higgins and Lee Rainwater, to the backing of CEPS and the Luxembourg government, and to the skill and hard work of all those who have worked on the LIS team. In contemplating all that has been involved, one cannot but be reminded of Thomas Alva Edison's definition of 'genius' as 'ninety-nine per cent perspiration'.

WHAT CAN ONE LEARN FROM CROSS-COUNTRY COMPARISONS?

There are those who are sceptical about the value of cross-country comparisons. Do they not raise as many questions as they answer? In responding to this criticism, the final chapter in this volume is helpful (as is a paper by a distinguished younger sceptic, D. Evilsad Vocate, also known as Stephen Jenkins, circulated in samizdat form during discussions of drafts of the chapters of this book). From the findings reported here, we find, for example, that measured income inequality is greater in the United States than in Sweden (Chapter 2), the Lorenz curve for family net income for the US being strictly below that for Sweden (Table 2.2). Similarly, we find that poverty, measured according to the economic distance standard (below half of median income) is greater in the US than in Sweden (Table 3.4). What can we learn from this?

First of all, we can learn nothing if the observed differences are due, not to a genuine difference in the distributions in the two countries, but to elements of non-comparability that remain between the two data sources. There is, for instance, the difference in the definition of the family unit discussed in Chapter 1. In the same way, the observed differences may be attributable, at least in part, to shortcomings of the data which apply to both countries but which have a differential impact, such as the under-representation of minority racial groups. The emphasis which is placed on data issues in the chapters in this book is therefore quite appropriate; and it is a significant benefit from access to the individual microdata that one can experiment with different ways in which the data can be brought closer to comparability.

Second, the observed differences may be the consequence of differences in the demographic structure of the countries. If, as in Chapter 4, we follow Seebohm Rowntree in regarding people as particularly likely to be in poverty at certain stages of the life cycle, then poverty rates will vary across countries according to the proportions of the population in these different stages. Differences are observed even if the distribution of life chances is the same. In this regard, the ability to decompose the data by sub-groups of the population, as is done in several chapters, is a valuable asset of the LIS database. As a reader of their results, one is still constrained by the tables that the investigators produced, but as a user of LIS it is possible to choose different cross-cuts of the survey data.

With the income distribution data on a comparable basis, and with account taken of differences in demographic structure, we may begin to draw lessons from the international comparisons. The potential is illustrated by the findings regarding poverty among the elderly. The results here (Chapters 4 and 5) suggest that there is virtually no poverty, measured by the half median standard, among the elderly in Sweden, whereas it is sizeable in the US and in the UK. Probing further, we find that the equivalent net incomes of the elderly, relative to the national mean, are no lower in the US than in Sweden (Table 4.4). What is different is degree of inequality among the elderly, which is remarkably low in Sweden and higher than that for the distribution as a whole in the US (as evidenced by the Gini coefficients in Table 4.5). It is not the total resources available to the elderly which appear to be crucial, but their distribution. This in turn suggests that a revenue-neutral policy could be devised to reduce poverty among the elderly: for example, by subjecting all retirement income to tax and using the proceeds to augment the benefits which go to all. In contrast, in the UK, inequality among the elderly, while greater than in Sweden, is less marked than in the US. It is the low average income of the elderly (for those aged 75+, only 67 per cent of the national average) which appears to be particularly responsible for their poverty in the UK.

International comparisons, by providing an alternative reference standard, suggest where domestic policy needs to be reconsidered. Can we go further and draw conclusions about the effectiveness of policy measures from the LIS comparisons? Sweden has a much higher ratio of taxes and transfers to total income than does the United States (Table 2.1). Is that why net incomes are less unequally distributed? Is it a matter of simple arithmetic? In fact, as the scatter of points in the top left-hand chart in Figure 4.2 indicates, other countries do not fit neatly along the Sweden/US line. And even if they did, the answer would be 'no', for a number of reasons. Aggregate measures of policy do not necessarily indicate their distributional impact, and the precise form of the policy differences needs to be investigated in detail. Differences in policy may lead to differences in gross incomes.

For example, the number of single-parent families, and hence the distribution of gross income, may depend on the scale of provision. As the public choice theorists will tell us, it may be that countries with relatively unequal distributions of gross income tend to elect governments which follow more conservative policies. Or perhaps both the distribution and the policies reflect more basic differences between the countries: a national 'fixed effect'. A prerequisite for coming to terms with these problems is a fully specified model of the relation between policy choices and the distribution of income.

Comparisons across countries may therefore provide useful indicators as to where domestic policy is in need of scrutiny, but there are limitations to what can be learned from straightforward comparisons of two or more countries without any explicit modelling of the policy differences. This leads us to consider the ways in which the LIS database may be developed.

DEVELOPING THE LIS DATABASE: A TIME-SERIES OF SURVEYS

One important respect in which it is planned to develop LIS is to add further 'waves' of data for the various countries, with the assembly of data for the mid 1980s being actively underway (see the Appendix). We will then have a time series of cross-sections.

The comparison now takes the form of a double difference:

$$\Delta_i \, \Delta_t$$

where the subscript i stands for country and the subscript t for time. What this means is that any national 'fixed effect' now disappears from the analysis. It may, for example, be the case that inequality in France is higher than in the UK for cultural or other reasons, but that if we compare the changes between 1989 and 1979 in the two countries we can learn about the different effects of Thatcher and Mitterrand. If inequality has fallen in France and risen in the UK, then this *may* provide evidence about the effectiveness of minimum wage legislation or of introducing a guaranteed minimum income.

At the same time, this double difference has to be interpreted with caution. The fixed effect may in fact be changing. The public choice theorist may say that the changes in government were not exogenous. The experience with panel data in other applications has brought out how taking differences may increase the sensitivity of the findings to measurement error. After all, the *changes* in inequality may be more sensitive to sampling errors and to other statistical problems. The analysis, and presentation, of the time series of cross-sections is going to require considerable care. Having said that, I feel that it is a quite logical development of the LIS database, and that it will be very interesting to see what it tells us about the differing experiences of the 1980s.

DEVELOPING THE LIS DATABASE: EXPLICIT TREATMENT OF DIFFERENCES IN POLICY

The second logical development is the explicit introduction of policy variables into the LIS database. The present papers contain interesting commentary on the role of differences in policy, for example those concerning benefits for single-parent families in Chapter 6, but the next step is to complement the survey data with a description of the key policy measures in each country. This should not simply be a verbal account. What is needed is a complementary database, containing policy parameters, which allows the net incomes to be calculated as a function of LIS variables and tax–benefit parameters. So child allowance V20 would be calculated as a function of LIS variables, such as D27 the number of children, and policy parameters such as the amount of child benefit. The construction of such a policy database, and particularly the mix of survey and calculated variables, requires a great deal of care, as has been found with the construction of tax-benefit models for individual countries (see Atkinson and Sutherland, 1988).

To construct tax–benefit models on a consistent basis for the LIS range of countries is a large task and again one has to ask what one would learn. Suppose that we are interested in the Gini coefficient, G, which depends on the vector of net incomes. Net incomes are obtained by applying the tax–benefit code, so that the vector of gross incomes $\mathbf{Y}$ becomes the vector of net incomes $N\{\mathbf{Y}\}$. If we attach a subscript, S, for Sweden, and B for Britain, then the conventional comparison is

$$G[\mathbf{N_B}\{\mathbf{Y_B}\}] \quad \text{with} \quad G[\mathbf{N_S}\{\mathbf{Y_S}\}]$$

In other words, we are changing both the distribution of gross incomes and the tax–benefit function. Differences in the Gini coefficient may arise from differences in the gross incomes, from differences in policy, or from the interaction between the two. Suppose, on the other hand, that we make the comparison

$$G[\mathbf{N_S}\{\mathbf{Y_B}\}] \quad \text{with} \quad G[\mathbf{N_B}\{\mathbf{Y_B}\}]$$

This holds constant the gross incomes and shows, in arithmetical terms, the impact of changing from the British to the Swedish tax–benefit code, isolating the differences in the tax–benefit calculations in the two countries. Such a calculation is helpful in answering the policy-relevant question for the British Cabinet – what would happen if we adopted certain features of the Swedish tax–benefit code? The LIS policy dataset is being used as a source of ideas about possible tax or benefit reform.

The above calculation is arithmetic. It ignores the interaction between the tax–benefit code and gross incomes. The change to Swedish levels of taxation and transfers may induce major changes in labour supply, savings behaviour or portfolio decisions. And the responses in Britain may be different from those in Sweden. It is conceivable that the differences across countries in the policies pursued reflect differential responses. Government may have the same objectives but be confronted with a different trade-off between equity and efficiency, on account of people being more responsive to taxation in one country than in the other. Or, to take another example, people in Sweden may be more willing to claim means-tested benefits than they are in Britain, for reasons no doubt located in history and culture. If this is so, then it may be 'cheaper' to devise an effective income support policy in Sweden, since greater reliance can be placed on means testing.

This points to the need for a third tier to the LIS database, including evidence about behavioural responses. The precise form that this should take is not clear to me at present. I believe that there are considerable difficulties in incorporating behavioural responses into policy analysis in a meaningful way, particularly where these have to cover a wide range of possible reactions, including such aspects as the propensity to claim benefits. For this reason, it may come later in the LIS development plan.

ENVOI

In this Introduction, I have tried to convey my enthusiasm about the LIS project – about what it has done and what it promises for the future. In the 1990s cross-national teams are going to play an increasing role in applied social science research, and LIS has shown us the way.

1 · THE LIS DATABASE: TECHNICAL AND METHODOLOGICAL ASPECTS

Timothy M. Smeeding and Günther Schmaus

INTRODUCTION

Over the past decade the use of household income survey data
in policy analysis has increased dramatically. Today the capacity
to describe the effects of existing policies and to simulate the
effects of changes in policy is well established in most modern
nations with elaborate welfare states. However, these analyses
tend to be parochial except for the fact that the techniques are
similar from country to country. The next step in improving
policy analysis can come from moving to a cross-national focus
using comparable income surveys in a number of countries. To
this end, the Luxembourg Income Study (LIS) constitutes a
databank of income surveys that can be used by scholars and
policy analysts to study the effects of different kinds of programmes
on poverty, income adequacy in retirement and the distribution
of economic well-being generally. The purpose of this chapter is
to introduce the reader to the technical and methodological issues
which were confronted in the course of preparing the LIS
database, and the courses adopted by the LIS project team. The
chapter begins with a brief historical overview of the LIS project.
The next section addresses the basic technical issues in arriving at
comparable datasets: definitional issues (dataset, year, population

1

coverage); income sharing units; income components and their definitions; and demographic variables and their definitions. A further section then discusses the important issue of data quality.

HISTORICAL OVERVIEW

The LIS project began in April 1983 under the sponsorship of the Government of Luxemburg. Its purpose was to gather, in one central location, sophisticated microdata sets containing comprehensive measures of income and economic well-being for a group of modern industrialized countries. The Centre for Population, Poverty, and Policy Studies (CEPS) and the International Networks for the Studies of Technology, Environment, Alternatives, and Development in Luxemburg (INSTEAD) were chosen as the central location.

The Luxemburg government originally sponsored and began the project to help promote networking between Luxemburg, surrounding countries, and the United States. Initially, the project director (Timothy Smeeding) and his technical assistant (Günther Schmaus) set up the data in conjunction with the dataset coordinators in each country. Those coordinators are by and large the authors of the chapters that follow. A set of papers was originally presented at a conference in 1985 in Luxemburg. The revised versions of these papers were revised and others added to produce this volume.

The project was thought promising enough to garner outside financial support. By late 1985 the Ford Foundation stepped in to help bridge the funding gap between the initial investment and joint funding on the part of a consortium of member countries. By 1986, the first member countries (Canada, Luxemburg, USA) had begun to support the database. The initial seven member countries on whose databases this book is based are Canada, Israel, Norway, Sweden, the United Kingdom, the United States, and West Germany. These countries were soon followed by others. By spring 1989 LIS had expanded to include ten countries, the initial seven plus Australia, Netherlands and Switzerland. Three additional countries (France, Italy and Poland) will be available for analysis early in 1990. Within the next two years several additional nations – including a Luxemburg database, plus

Belgium, Finland, Greece, Austria and Hungary – are expected to join as well. At this writing a second round of datasets for the 1986–7 period is being mounted to the LIS databank, permitting comparisons over time as well as across countries. The Appendix contains additional information about the LIS database and how to gain access to it.

BASIC TECHNICAL ISSUES

In order to produce the final harmonised LIS dataset, a range of adjustment procedures were required. This section reviews these procedures, indicating the strengths, weaknesses and limitations of each dataset and procedure.

Definitional issues

The LIS procedure began with each country dataset expert filling out a database questionnaire which indicated the size, comprehensivity of population coverage and detail of income components for each possible dataset. Each respondent listed what he or she thought were the major strengths or weaknesses of these datasets for the type of comparative social policy analyses to which LIS is intended to contribute. The criteria for accepting a dataset were several, and trade-offs were often made in order to arrive at a representative sample of datasets and countries. Still, several datasets were not up to standard and were, for one reason or another, excluded.

Most important for each acceptable dataset was substantial detail related to income by source, especially public transfer income. In order to provide a flexible tool for analysis of the workings of the welfare state, this was the most crucial item. Also of concern was the timeliness of the dataset (i.e. nearness to 1979 – the target year for the surveys[1]), its quality (as measured by response rates and other indicators of non-sampling error), its size, the income accounting unit and geographical location. On the other hand, trepidation concerning just who was in the project team and what LIS was all about led some governments to forbid export of suitable datasets to the LIS project centre. It is hoped to add such datasets to LIS in the near future now that the first results of the project are visible. A final pair of overriding constraints were time and budget.

Some of the datasets include the results of additional analyses as well as the original survey data. For example, the US tape includes Smeeding's (1982) estimates of the value of in-kind benefits, while the UK tape includes the official Central Statistical Office estimates of the incidence of certain indirect taxes, subsidies and benefits-in-kind. However, only the original data were incorporated in the version included in the database, and thus in the analyses reported in this book. Comparative investigation of the distribution of indirect taxes and non-cash benefits within the LIS framework must await a further stage of the project.

Table 1.1 contains an overview of the datasets which are contained in the LIS database and are reported on here, giving the dataset name and size, income year, sampling frame and population representativeness. All datasets contain detailed information on income (by source), taxes and household or family composition. All but the Canadian and West German datasets are for 1979; these two are for 1981.[2] All but West Germany, Norway and the United Kingdom collect annual survey income data. The UK income data come from an expenditure or budget survey, while the Norwegian data come from a sample of income tax files.[3] In the United Kingdom and West Germany, weekly and monthly data on earnings and usual income sources are collected along with some types of annual income (dividends, royalties, profits, etc.). The data are then adjusted to annual income terms based on length of time unemployed, retired, etc. Each country has considerable experience with this method (Ramprakash, 1975; Stephenson, 1980) and, subject to certain well-known limitations of virtually all survey income data sources (e.g. O'Higgins, 1980), these UK and West German data compare well with annual income estimates from other sources.

The datasets vary considerably in sample size with the very large US and Canadian datasets allowing for quite detailed income and demographic breakdowns, while the smaller West German and Israeli datasets are problematic when examining certain specific groups, e.g. particular types of elderly (see Chapter 5) and one-parent families (see Chapter 6). Finally, all the datasets exclude the institutionalised and the homeless, thus reducing the sample frame to about 97 or 98 per cent of the national

Table 1.1 An overview of LIS datasets

Country	Data set name, income year (and size)[1]	Population coverage[3]	Sampling frame[8]
United States	*Current Population Survey*, 1979 (69,000)	97.5[4]	Decennial census
Israel	*Family Expenditure Survey*, 1979 (2,300)	89.0[5]	Electoral register
Norway	*Norwegian tax files*, 1979 (10,400)	98.5[4]	Tax records
Canada	*Survey of Consumer Finances*, 1981 (37,900)	97.5[4]	Decennial census
United Kingdom	*Family Expenditure Survey*,[2] 1979 (6,900)	96.5[6]	Electoral register
West Germany	*Transfer Survey*, 1981[2] (2,800)	91.5[7]	Electoral register
Sweden	*Swedish Income Distribution – Living Survey*, 1979 (9,600)	98.0[4]	Electoral register

1. Number of actual household units surveyed.
2. The UK and West German surveys collect sub-annual income data which is normalised to annual income levels. See text for explanation.
3. As a per cent of total national population.
4. Excludes institutionalised and homeless populations.
5. Excludes rural population (those living in places of 2,000 or less), institutionalised, homeless, people in kibbutzim and guest-workers.
6. Excludes those not on the electoral register, the homeless and the institutionalised.
7. Excludes households with foreign-born heads, the institutionalised and the homeless.
8. Sampling frame indicates the universe from which the relevant household population sample was drawn.

population. When measuring poverty or low income this may prove problematic (Atkinson, 1985). In addition the Israeli data exclude the rural population and those living in kibbutzim; while the West German dataset excludes foreign heads of household. Again one should be aware of these differences in examining relative poverty and employment status across countries. However, comparisons of Israeli poverty and income inequality with urban poverty and income inequality in two of our sample countries resulted in no difference in rank order between these two countries. Documentation on the effects of uncounted illegal aliens or differential census undercount of particular groups (e.g. blacks in the United States) is not available.

The data reported here are the first such data that are comparable across countries. This characteristic makes them uniquely valuable for analysis even though they are nearly a decade old.

Income sharing units

One crucial element in comparing the composition of incomes within one country, much less across several countries, is the issue of income accounting (e.g. see Fiegehen and Lansley, 1975). Table 1.2 presents the situation with respect to the LIS countries. Since flexibility of data use is a prime goal for LIS, ideally the choice of 'family' (all persons living together who are related by blood, marriage or adoption) vs. 'household' (all persons, related or unrelated, who share the same living arrangements) should be left to the researcher and to the research problem at hand. However, this was not always feasible for this cohort of data. Since the size of the family or household unit is known for all datasets, the person can always be used as the unit of analysis.[4]

Table 1.2 indicates that, with minor exceptions, all datasets contain family data, while only five contain household data.[5] Four datasets contain both. The anomalies are listed in the last footnote to the table.

The differences are significant, though for the analysis reported here we are confident that the figures for Sweden are comparable with those of the other countries. The Norwegian family is very close to the LIS family definition except for the grouping together of unmarried persons with those whom they support (or by whom they are supported). Because the rationale of mutual income support is ultimately the objective of defining income sharing units in the first place, the Norwegian family definition, which is based on mutual support regardless of marital status, may, in principle, be superior to the standard family definition given above.

In Sweden, the major problem is that of adult children (e.g. students) who are listed as separate families even if they live with their parents and siblings in the same household. In fact, if poverty is defined as having an equivalent disposable income less than half of median equivalent disposable income (see Chapter 3),

Table 1.2 Income-sharing units

Country	Household[1]	Family[2]	Both
Canada	X	X	X
West Germany[3]	X	X	X
Israel[3]	X	X	
Norway[4]		X	
Sweden[4]		X	
United Kingdom	X	X	X
United States	X	X	X

1. 'Household': one or more persons whether related or unrelated who share common living quarters.
2. 'Family': two or more persons living together (sharing common living quarters) who are related by blood, marriage or adoption, or a single individual not living with relatives. One-person families are often termed 'unrelated individuals', but for the sake of simplicity they are termed (one-person) families here.
3. In Israel and West Germany, multiple family households can be identified but, at least in the case of Israel, income sources or amounts cannot be separated among family members within a given household. Note that only 2.4 per cent of West German households and 2.2 per cent of Israeli households have multiple families.
4. The Norwegian and Swedish families differ slightly from the family definition given in 2 above. The Norwegian 'family' is best defined by Radner (1985) as: 'All persons who lived in the same dwelling and had the same surname are grouped in the same family. However, one family never comprises more than one married couple. Spouses are grouped in the same family and dependants are grouped together with their supporters regardless of their surname.' Since 1972 (when the Swedish family definition was identical to the definition above) the Swedish family has been defined as 'either two adults who have lived, or normally should have lived, at least half the income year in the same dwelling irrespective of marital status and with or without children; or a single adult with or without children'. (Adults are considered to be persons 18 years of age or more.)

62,000 or 15.1 per cent of the 410,000 poor persons in Sweden are single persons aged 18–24 who were in full-time education at the time of the survey. The overall poverty rate of 5.0 per cent in Sweden would fall to 4.2 per cent were all such students treated as non-poor on the usual family income definition basis. However, without knowing how many of these persons actually live with or are otherwise supported by other persons, one cannot be sure that they are non-poor.

Of course, given the microdata basis of LIS, the researcher is free to follow any one of several paths in dealing with these units' problems:

1. Only the three (five) countries with completely consistent family (household) definitions could be utilised. This would exclude Norway and Sweden at the least, were the household definition used, and Israel and West Germany as well, were the very strict family definition used.
2. Only consistently defined single family households could be utilised including all countries but Sweden and Norway, but excluding multi-family households in all remaining countries.
3. Persons in families, or families per se (with the exceptions noted above), could be utilised, including all countries.

The general assumption in this book is that the differences in family definitions are not so severe as to preclude the third option, which was therefore chosen. However, the database is constructed so that each LIS researcher can make his or her own decision of which countries to include or exclude, and on what income accounting unit basis. Enough countries have now been added to LIS so that researchers can now select a fully consistent subset of countries for analysis.

Income definitions

One major task faced by LIS was to aggregate (or to disaggregate) country-specific income elements into internationally consistent income categories. Table 1.3 contains basic income variable aggregations and definitions. Before describing these income aggregations, however, it should be stressed that international comparability and consistency rather than perfection are the goals. For instance, the imputed rental value for owner-occupied homes is defined differently for each country with such information. Alternatively, home value is consistently defined across five datasets. Thus a researcher could, for instance, consistently define implicit rental values as some percentage of home value across the five datasets containing this information. This procedure would in effect ignore each country's own preferred implicit rental formula in favour of a definition that is consistent across all datasets.

Table 1.3 Basic LIS income variable definitions: aggregation and component variables

Aggregation	Component variables
A1 wages and salaries	V1 (wage and salary income)
A2 self-employment income (SEI)	V4 (farm SEI) and V5 (non-farm SEI)
A3 earned income	A1 + A2
A4 cash property income	V8 (interest, rents, dividends, royalties, annuities, etc.)
A5 factor income	A3 + A4
A6 payroll taxes[2]	V7 (payroll taxes on SEI) + V13 (employment payroll taxes)
A7 direct taxes[1]	V11 (personal income tax) + A6
A8 social insurance transfers[4]	V16 (sick pay) + V17 (accident pay) + V22 (maternity pay) + V23 (military or war-related benefits) + V24 (other cash or near-cash social insurance)
A9 means-tested transfers[4]	V25 (cash payments) + V26 (near-cash payments)
A10 public cash transfers	A8 + A9
A11 employment-related pensions	V32 (private sector employment-related pensions) + V33 (public sector employment-related pensions)
A12 private transfers	V34 (alimony and child support) + V35 (regular private transfers)
A13 other income	A11 + A12 + V36 (other cash income)
A14 gross income	A5 + A10 + A13
A15 disposable (net) income	A14 − A7
A16 retirement income[3]	A11 + V19 (social retirement)
A17 market income	A5 + A11

1. With respect to direct taxes, personal property or wealth taxes (V12) are not counted as direct taxes, nor is the West German church tax (which is reported as V14, other tax, in the Appendix). Because the proportion of property taxes on renters cannot be separately estimated (owing to the uncertain incidence of the property tax), property taxes on owner-occupied homes (or other durables) are not subtracted. Church taxes are considered voluntary uses of income.
2. Employer payroll taxes are also available (V2). Some researchers may want to define gross wages and salaries to include employer payroll taxes because of the differential mix between employer and employee payroll taxes across countries, and because in the case of payroll taxes on self-employment income

continued over page

Table 1.3 continued

(V7), both the employee and employer portion are by definition deducted. Still, the definition of disposable net income (A15 in Table 1.3) is net of all types of payroll tax.
3. Retirement income (A16 in Table 1.3) is defined to include employment-related pensions (V32 and V33) and social retirement pensions (V19). Because both types of pensions are funded by employment-related contributions, either voluntary or involuntary (payroll taxes), on both employer and employee, it may often be best simply to work with aggregate retirement income. In Sweden, for instance, social security retirement and occupational pensions for government workers cannot be separated. Since the public sector in Sweden is so large, this differentiation may prove difficult when comparing the role of occupational pension with the role of social retirement.
4. The basic distinctions in transfer payments are between social insurance (or non-means-tested) transfers and means-tested benefits; and between cash and non-cash transfers. Within this classification system, however, a category of near-cash transfers has also been defined (V24 if not means tested, or V26 if means tested). Near-cash benefits include all forms of transfers that are, in a strict sense, in-kind payments (i.e. they are tied to a specific requirement such as school attendance) but have a cash equivalent value equal to the market value. In effect these are disguised cash transfers. For instance, in the United States this includes food stamps which substitute food vouchers for cash payments that would have otherwise been made. In West Germany this category includes cash student allowances (which require school attendance and are means tested on the incomes of parents, students and spouses of students). In the United Kingdom, Sweden and West Germany, it includes cash allowances to help reduce rental housing costs. In West Germany, if cash student allowances were not means tested, they would be recorded under scholarships in V24. Moreover, V24 may include other non-means-tested near-cash benefits such as training allowances. In contrast, in the United States and West Germany, public housing benefits (i.e. for those living in a publicly owned housing unit at below market rent) are not included here. Instead, they are treated as non-cash transfers (V27) because they do not have a cash equivalent value equal to their market value. Of course, this is a fairly subjective area, and if there is any doubt that the cash equivalent value did not equal the market value, the transfer was counted as non-cash transfer (V27, V28, V29 or V31) and not as near-cash transfer (V24 or V26).

At this stage, LIS has concentrated on annual cash income components. Non-cash income, wealth, consumption, savings and other indicators of well-being (e.g. subjective feelings on well-offness, health indicators and neighbourhood amenities) are not dealt with in any great detail. In a further stage of LIS, it is planned to broaden the income definitions to include at least basic components of non-money income such as food, housing, health care and education.

Gross wage and salary income and hourly wage and salary income are separately reported for family or household heads or spouses. For the most part these variables are obtained by dividing reported wage and salary income by reported hours worked, and so they are rough estimates of average hourly earnings.

As is always the case with income survey data, negative or zero incomes sometimes result. For instance, negative incomes may appear in cases where large business losses swamp modest positive income amounts. Overall zero incomes are usually because there was no response about income, since virtually all households have some positive cash income. Each researcher is left to deal with zero or negative incomes as he or she sees fit. For six countries the percentage of families with zero or negative incomes ranged from 0 per cent (Israel) to 1.1 per cent (United States); West Germany is the outlier, having 2.7 per cent of all families with zero incomes.[6]

The income aggregations in Table 1.3 conform to basic United Nations Statistical Guidelines (1977) with little variation. A number of detailed points about these variable aggregations are set out in the notes to Table 1.3. Appendix Table A.1 presents a complete list of income variables.

Demographic variables

The sociodemographic variables common across LIS countries include information on the household or family (size, location, tenure, number of earners, number of children, etc.), data on the household (family) head or spouse (age, sex, marital status, industry, period of employment, work status, etc.) and variables on occupation, education and disability.[7] If a country dataset contained a country-specific definition of poverty, it was also added to the dataset. Appendix Table A.2 presents a complete list of demographic variables.

It is important to note that not all variables are available for all countries. For instance, if maternity/paternity allowances (V22) are important to the analysis, they can only be separately identified in the United Kingdom, Israel and Sweden. In Norway, West Germany and Canada they cannot be efficiently separated from wages.

Almost all countries contain a great deal of information on income, especially public transfer income. All major forms of regular cash income are reported on all surveys. In general, direct taxes are also well reported (except for mandatory employee contributions – or payroll taxes – in Canada). As noted earlier, there is only sparse non-cash benefit data available at this stage of LIS.

Equivalent income

Several papers employ the concept of equivalent income, whereby cash income is adjusted by the number of equivalent adults in a family in order to construct a measure of the level of economic welfare or the standard of living available to a family. While significantly different scales have been developed based on budget studies (van der Gaag and Smolensky, 1982), expert judgements of the income necessary to meet minimum standards (Orshansky, 1965) and on subjective measures of well-being (van Praag *et al.*, 1982) there is no consensus on either the 'best' method, or on the most appropriate relativities as between households of different sizes and compositions.

The analyses presented in this book are, therefore, based on a rather simpler strategy designed to capture the broad effects of adjusting income using equivalence scales. The scales used allocate a weight of 0.5 to the first individual in any unit, a value of 0.25 for each individual from the second to the ninth (so that a nine-person unit has an equivalence factor of 2.5), and a value of 3.0 to those few units with 10 or more members. Each unit's equivalent income was then calculated by dividing its measured income by the appropriate equivalence factor.

DATA QUALITY

One of the most crucial elements of comparison among countries' income datasets is relative data quality. Non-sampling errors in surveys are often many and complex. Overall survey response errors, income non-response and net income underreporting are all of concern. The discussion here concentrates only on the latter two problems.[8]

Comparative income studies are critically dependent on relative overall and item-specific data quality. Unless the degree of response and net reporting errors are relatively similar, it is difficult to make accurate comparisons of income inequality or relative income positions of various groups. For instance, if one particular type of income is underreported more than another type, and if that income type is critically related to the overall degree of inequality (e.g. property income or self-employment income) or to the relative income position of, say, the elderly vs. the non-elderly (e.g. occupational pensions) cross-national comparisons may be quite misleading. For this reason, it is important to discuss the issue of relative income data quality.

Table 1.4 represents five conceptual levels of income reporting, and indicates the level at which each LIS country dataset lies. The least complete income concept is that in the bottom row – the amount of income actually reported by the population, excluding entire non-interviews but leaving partial or item non-response intact (row 5). Currently only the West German data are in this state.[9] The next step is edited income (row 4), whereby all item non-response is corrected for (i.e. there are no more income non-responses). These adjustments may take many forms: 'hot-deck' imputation (United States), 'cold-deck' imputation (West Germany) or limited comparisons to administrative records

Table 1.4 Differential income data quality: a conceptual breakdown

Row	Income concept	Differences	LIS country dataset
1.	True income		
		Unrecorded income	
2.	Administrative record income		
		Tax cheating	
3.	Tax reported income	....	(Norway)
		Reporting error	
4.	Edited survey income	....	(United States, United Kingdom, Sweden, Canada, Israel)
		Item non-response	
5.	Reported survey income	....	(West Germany)

(Sweden).[10] The US, Canadian, Swedish, UK and Israeli data are in this condition.

The in-between category in row 3 is the amount of income recorded by tax-based surveys, and the Norwegian data are at this (row 3) level. While not all survey income sources are taxable in all countries, it is assumed that taxes are more reliably reported than are survey incomes, as is the usual case (Radner, 1983). The tax-based records in row 3 are presumably incomplete due to tax evasion, and are thus assumed to be less accurate than the administrative data represented in the second row. In such data, incomes are grossed up to the total amount recorded by some administrative intermediary, usually and preferably national income accounts or administrative records of government agencies. The differences between the top row, true income, and the administrative amounts are usually due to those amounts of income which are not recorded by the national accounts at all. Because no dataset records true income, the critical income level is the second highest one, the administrative level.

Three additional comments are in order. First, in some countries, national income accounts may not be all that much better than survey data. That is, the quality of the administrative data may be in some question to begin with. For instance, wage and salary income in the Canadian Survey of Consumer Finances amount to 101.6 per cent of the comparable National Accounts estimate (see Table 1.5).

Secondly, before survey (or tax) data can be compared with administrative data, the latter must be adjusted to produce estimates of identical income concepts and populations. That is, administrative data are often gross of income amounts which are not relevant when estimating income (e.g. see income variable V37). Also, income received by those households not in the survey population (e.g. non-residents, the deceased and the institutionalised) must be adjusted for. These adjustments are crucial. For instance, Atkinson and Micklewright (1982) show that the 1977 comparable British 'Blue Book' (National Account) estimate of occupational pensions is only £3.4 billion, or 55 per cent of the total administrative amount (£6.1 billion) once these adjustments are made.

Finally, rows 3, 4 and 5 are based on microdata, while row 2 amounts are based on aggregate or macrodata. Thus, if one finds, for instance, that in the United States total wages and salaries are 97.4 per cent of the adjusted administrative amount, this does not mean that all individuals have reported 97.4 per cent of their true wages and salaries. So it must be stressed that overall readings of data quality (e.g. those in Table 1.5) do not provide all the necessary ingredients for adjusting microdata for reporting errors (see Radner, 1983). In particular they do not allow the researcher to differentiate between non-reporting and under-reporting (or overreporting) of individual income amounts.

Unfortunately, comparisons of survey data with adjusted administrative record data are currently available for only three LIS countries. These comparisons, for Canada, the United Kingdom and the United States, are shown in Table 1.5. In all three countries item non-response on survey income has been

Table 1.5 Quality of income data for three countries: ratio of survey estimates to adjusted administrative data estimates

	Country and year		
Income item	Canada (1981)[1] (%)	United Kingdom (1977)[2] (%)	United States (1979)[3] (%)
Wages and salaries	101.6	92.8	97.4
Self-employment income	78.2	75.7	84.2
Property income	60.5	55.3	45.1
Occupational pension income	85.4	83.9	81.5
Government transfers	77.5	96.2	82.8
All income[4]	92.4	89.8	89.0

1. Canada survey data from *Survey of Consumer Finances* for 1981; comparisons from unpublished tabulations based on family income data provided by Gail Oja, former director of Income Statistics, Statistics Canada.
2. UK survey data from Family Expenditure Survey for 1977; comparisons as reported by Atkinson and Micklewright (1982) using in part a methodology developed by Ramprakash (1975).
3. US survey data from the Current Population Survey for 1979; comparisons as reported in US Bureau of the Census (1981, Table A-2).
4. Based on sum of items presented above only. Some income amounts, e.g. alimony and child support or private transfers, have no administrative data to which the survey data can be compared.

adjusted for, and reported income amounts have been weighted up to national population estimates.[11] The Canadian and US surveys are based on annual data, while the UK data are based on monthly data that has been analysed by a sophisticated normalisation procedure (see Ramprakash, 1975).

Overall income estimates are about 90 per cent of national income totals in all three surveys. However, specific item estimates often differ by some non-trivial degree. In the UK, earnings are reported only at 92.8 per cent rate, despite the fact that pay receipts are consulted in about 75 per cent of all cases (Kemsley et al., 1980). Most probably these differences reflect either non-reported secondary income (which may also be part of unreported tax income) or biases in the UK methodology for adjusting monthly earnings and/or unemployment to annual totals. The Canadian amounts are actually larger than the adjusted national account totals, indicating either poor national account totals or survey sample weighting problems. Self-employment income reporting also differs substantially across surveys, though as Atkinson and Micklewright (1982) suggest, it is often hard to estimate just what is meant by 'self-employment income' either in surveys or in the national accounts. However, because self-employment is less than 7.5 per cent of total income in all three countries, this problem is not so great as it might be.[12]

Property income reporting plagues virtually all types of income surveys and the three reported here are no different in this respect. Because of its highly skewed distribution by income and by age, this differential reporting problem is to be carefully noted. For instance, adjustments for non-reporting of all types of income among the elderly in the 1973 US Current Population Survey, based on a record for record match with several sources of administrative data, indicate that the overall incomes of the elderly would increase by 37 per cent were it accurately reported, as compared to about 9 per cent for the population as a whole (Radner, 1983). Most of this differential was due to property income non-reporting among the high income elderly.

While occupational pension income is consistently reported across all three surveys, transfer income also differs substantially. Again, this time because of the pro-poor nature of transfer income, one must carefully note these differences. While the United Kingdom monthly data do a much better job of overall transfer income reporting than do the other annual income-based surveys, there is some evidence of misreporting of transfer income by transfer type (Atkinson and Micklewright, 1982). Also while the US overall transfer income reporting rate is 82.8 per cent, means-tested benefits are only about 75 per cent reported (Smeeding, 1982, Appendix F). In Canada, social assistance, provincial income supplements and provincial tax credits which are also largely means tested are only about 50 per cent reported.

These differences must be carefully noted when comparing relative incomes across countries. For instance because of the coexistence of relatively better reporting of property income and relatively worse reporting of transfer income, overall measures of income inequality in Canada may be upwardly biased compared to those in other countries.

CONCLUSIONS

This chapter describes the background and technical issues related to the construction of the LIS database. The specific procedures used and problems encountered have been highlighted in some detail because of the novelty of what LIS is attempting. This degree of detail allows the reader and potential database user to understand both the components that make up the LIS database and the quality and comparability of the data. In subsequent chapters, the database is used to present new comparative estimates of aspects of poverty and resource distribution in these seven countries.

NOTES

We would like to thank the Ford Foundation, the Government of Luxemburg, the special Collaborative Programme 3 at the University of Frankfurt and Computer Resources Incorporated (CRI) for their support in completing this project. We would like to thank Alfred Kahn and Sheila Kamerman for helpful comments on specific elements of the LIS dataset and also Richard Hauser and Michael O'Higgins for clarification and comment.

1. The year 1979 was chosen because only 1979 data were available for Norway, while the 1979 USA Current Population Survey (CPS)

dataset offered a considerable breadth of tax and non-cash income sources not found in other CPSs.

2. Because the 1981–83 recession was only beginning in 1982, differences in exogenous economic conditions in data years should have little influence on the outcome of the study. While West Germany's unemployment rate for 1981, 5.3 per cent, was somewhat above that in 1979, it is widely thought that the group most subject to this phenomenon, guest-workers, are largely excluded from the West German dataset.

3. In Norway because of the comprehensivity of the income tax base, 99.2 per cent of personal money income is subject to tax. In some countries, where income transfers are largely not taxed, the income tax base is at best a partial measure of economic status. But in Norway, only local government welfare and unemployment benefits are excluded from the income tax base.

4. This requires the assumption of equal intrahousehold or intrafamily income sharing (but see Lazear and Michael, 1984). Because none of the datasets contains individual income receipts for all individuals *within* the family, 'true' individual incomes are not generally known. The one exception is earnings and other sociodemographic data for the household head and/or spouse.

5. When dealing with the family unit of analysis, household-based income transfers (e.g. near-cash housing allowances in several countries or Food Stamps in the United States) are prorated according to relative family size within the household. Thus in a household with one three-person family and one single-person family, the former would receive 75 per cent of the benefit and the latter 25 per cent.

6. In the West German case, the large majority of these records are for elderly persons who report little or no cash incomes. Each author dealt with this problem based on then available demographic (age, family size, etc.) data concerning these records. The West German datafile has since been edited for total income non-response before the data were made available for wider public use.

7. These variables have not all been consistently coded and may require some additional work by interested researchers. However, given the separate codebooks for each country dataset, this work should not be terribly time-consuming.

8. Overall survey response rates are in the 70–95 per cent range, except for the Israel survey which has only a 50 per cent response rate.

9. Of the total 2,975 West German family income records, 54 had severe income non-response problems which required later adjustments. The contributors to this book were apprised of the difficulties, and individual adjustments (e.g. not counting these records and reweighting, or imputing income amounts) have been made in each chapter.

10. In Sweden only some non-response items, e.g. transfer income, are directly compared to administrative registers. In other cases, non-

response adjustments take other forms. 'Hot-decking' imputation in the United States is done by finding the nearest record to the non-response based on several criteria (age, sex, family size, etc.) and assigning the amount reported in that record to the non-response. Cold-decking is accomplished by calculating average amounts for those reporting an income type by age, sex and other income levels, and assigning the average amount to the non-respondent.

11. In the United Kingdom there are no 'official' population weights. The sample is randomly selected from election registers. However, there is differential overall survey non-response by age and region. The income totals here have been weighted to reflect differential survey response rates by age. See Atkinson and Micklewright (1982).

12. In other countries with high self employment income, from either farm or non-farm sources as a proportion of national income, e.g. France or Italy, this problem is much more serious.

2 · INCOME DISTRIBUTION AND REDISTRIBUTION: A Microdata Analysis for Seven Countries

Michael O'Higgins, Günther Schmaus and Geoffrey Stephenson

INTRODUCTION

Most comparisons of the distribution and redistribution of income across countries have had to rely on using already-published data, a procedure which has a range of readily apparent weaknesses. Such data are presented in groups which may vary from country to country, and may differ from the groupings which might be desired by any particular researcher. Their choice of income concept and of income unit may be similarly variable and unsuitable, and the issues of how to rank incomes and how to weight both income and the income unit are rarely mentioned. The restrictions imposed by pre-structured data both distort empirical comparisons and render almost futile (and, therefore, often neglected) any methodological discussion; at most, methodological issues tend to be raised as apologetic caveats rather than in the context of analytical choices. The effects of some of these weaknesses may be illustrated by outlining some of the limitations imposed by then-available data on the much-quoted OECD study carried out by Sawyer (1976).

According to his account, Sawyer had to derive pre-tax data for Canada, West Germany and Sweden by adding the average amount of tax paid within income classes to post-tax data.

Similarly he had to derive post-tax data for France, Japan, the United Kingdom and the United States by deducting average tax payments from pre-tax data (procedures in which, as he acknowledges, 'inequality tends to be underestimated since households have not been [re]ranked by the derived income concept' (1976, p. 12)). This procedure also means that the income variation within income classes is not captured in summary measures of inequality.

Furthermore, in his data for some countries (such as Norway), certain taxes deducted at source (e.g. employee social security contributions) were not included in the pre-tax income concept, so that the data actually represented an intermediate income stage between the pre- and post-tax concepts. In addition, 'many of the estimates are subject to . . . error arising from interpolation' (1976, p. 12) since the published data had to be rearranged (for example, from fixed-interval income classes) in order to be presented in the common form of decile shares.

Finally, it may be noted that while Sawyer attempts to take account of the impact of differences in household size and composition on the distribution of economic welfare, his transformations are apparently based on adjustments within pre-structured income classes[1] and, although he comments on the impact of such transformations on the identity of the people in the various deciles, no information, apart from a slight Swedish example, is actually given on the identities of those in the various deciles after such transformations – presumably because the data could not be reordered so as to permit this.

More recently, as microdata have become available, some international comparisons have involved individual researchers in different countries trying to derive comparable concepts from their own microdata sets. On the basis of such separately gathered data, joint analyses have been carried out (see, for example, Smolensky et al., 1979; Ruggles and O'Higgins, 1981; O'Higgins and Ruggles, 1981).

LIS seeks to move beyond these approaches by gathering sets of microdata for different countries, and reorganising these data so that they conform to certain common standards, concepts and structures. This does not, of course, mean that every item in every tape is rendered comparable; it does mean that if LIS variable X exists on the tape for country A, it should be comparable to variable X on any other country tape. While it is not possible to create a complete set of common variables, each represented on every tape, it is possible to ensure that such basic items as gross income, factor income and cash income, or per capita, equivalent or unadjusted income, are defined to common standards.

This chapter reports the results, in respect of international comparisons of income distribution and redistribution, of a first stage of the LIS project. Microdata tapes for seven countries – Canada, the United States, the United Kingdom, West Germany, Sweden, Norway and Israel – have been organised in the manner summarised above, and described in more detail in Chapter 1. As the later parts of this chapter demonstrate, the use of consistently organised microdata allows comparisons of inequality in respect of similarly defined variables, permits methodological alternatives to be used to indicate data sensitivity to such alternatives, and allows the countries to be compared on aspects of income ranking and policy equity in ways which would not be possible without consistently organised microdata.

While the database has been described in the previous chapter, a number of important issues of methodology should be discussed.

METHODOLOGICAL ISSUES IN THE LIS ANALYSES OF INCOME DISTRIBUTION

As argued earlier, issues of methodology often bear little relation to issues of data analysis in international income distribution studies because the available data simply do not allow presentational choices based on methodological preferences. In this case, however, not only was such choice possible, it was essential in order to deal with the mass of data presented by the availability of seven relatively consistent microdata sets: whilst the tapes had been rendered consistent, this had deliberately been done in a way which left methodological decisions to the individual researcher. This variety led to what Stark has termed an international learning process:

> We came across many different concepts, locations of data, methods of collection etc. These created quite a long period of learning and familiarisation . . . . Whilst standardisation of the precise meaning

of concepts would be very valuable it is to be hoped that this would not lead to the restriction in the variety of concepts. An 'international learning process' undoubtedly encompasses the benefits of comprehending income distributions beyond the normal presentation available in any one country (1977, p. 2).

The major methodological issues may be summarised as relating to the measures of income, the unit value of the income, the weighting of the units in measuring inequality and the method by which income units were ranked in order to create an income hierarchy prior to measuring inequality. Each will be discussed in turn.

The measure of income

The analysis in the chapter focuses on two primary measures of income – gross income and net cash income. Gross income is close to the US concept of total money income, and to Sawyer's (1976) concept of pre-tax income. It includes all income from employment and self-employment, property income, occupational pensions, state and private cash transfers, as well as other cash incomes. The sum of employment, self-employment and property incomes is labelled factor income, and market income is factor income plus occupational pensions. Net cash income is gross income less direct taxes (both income taxes and employee social insurance levies), and is similar to Sawyer's post-tax income concept.

Many previous inequality analyses, particularly those with a focus on income redistribution, have chosen a concept of 'original' or pre-transfer income as the primary income concept, and then gone on to use this as a base or counterfactual against which to measure the redistributive impact of transfers or taxes. While measures of pre-transfer income are relevant to those whose immediate policy concern is to examine how and from whom transfer payments could be financed, their use as a counterfactual appears to assume that in the absence of government tax and transfer programmes, the income distribution would be as represented by the 'original' or market distribution.

Plainly this is not the case, particularly when some of the government programmes (e.g. pensions) have existed for so long that individuals have taken them into account when planning and anticipating their future income needs. In addition, since some of the 'market' income may be mandated by government legislation (e.g. sickness absence payments in West Germany, some pension provision in the United Kingdom), the distinction is inaccurate even as a static separation of the transfer and pre-transfer elements of gross income. Since different countries have chosen different balances of governmental direct transfers, in-kind provision, mandating and regulation in their social programmes, such a distinction could be especially inaccurate in a comparative study. Furthermore, government programmes themselves affect the distribution of factor income, even in a static analysis, through the incomes which they pay to service providers, such as doctors and teachers, rendering the pre-transfer measure even less appropriate as a counterfactual.[2]

The use of gross income as the first main income concept avoids these difficulties by allowing prior elements of income to be examined in terms either of their own distribution or of their contributions to gross income in different parts of the distribution, without making any assumptions about what the distribution might otherwise have been.

The use of net cash income is slightly more problematical. Whilst the counterfactual problem is less significant (though not totally absent – the shape of the gross distribution may be affected by the pre-existing structure of taxation), governments may and do alter the balance between direct and indirect taxes in their revenue-raising. Some differences between countries in these results may therefore reflect such policy choices, since the LIS analyses do not at this stage take any account of indirect taxes. However, comparisons of the distribution of gross incomes are affected by the different balances between employer and employee social insurance contributions and payroll taxes in different countries (since gross income only includes employee contributions), whereas net cash incomes are not affected by this policy choice. The balance between direct and indirect taxes may, therefore, affect the explanation of the net cash data, but not their accuracy as measures of the distribution of 'spendable' income in the different countries. In other words, whilst comparisons of gross and net cash income are only limited and qualified measures of the impact of taxation, the net cash measure clearly portrays an important stage in the process of income distribution.

The unit value of the income

The units in which people live, and the income of which is therefore measured, differ in size and composition. This gives rise, as Atkinson notes, to two important questions:

> First, how should we adjust measured income to obtain a comparable, or 'equivalent', indicator of welfare? Second, how should we weight income units of different sizes when making judgements about overall dispersion? (1983, p. 48).

Whilst per capita income is sometimes used to adjust measured income, a measure of equivalent income – the standard of living available to each member of the unit, assuming income pooling – better represents the level of economic welfare which each unit's measured income allows it. This raises the question of determining the equivalence factor – the relationship between measured income and standard of living – for units of varying sizes and compositions. Two related questions are salient here:

1. What equivalence scale is appropriate for each dataset?
2. Should a common scale be used across the seven countries?

In principle, the answer to the second question is 'no': the relationship between levels of economic welfare and income level, unit size and composition is prima facie likely to differ from country to country (and over time in any one country). However, to use a different scale for each country would be to invite the response that any inter-country differences emerging in the consequent results simply reflected these equivalence scale differences. Whilst sensitivity analyses would overcome such responses, it was decided to use a common scale for this analysis. As indicated in the previous chapter, the chosen scale allocated a value of 0.50 to the first individual in any unit, a value of 0.25 for each individual from the second to the ninth (so that a nine-person unit had an equivalence factor of 2.5), and a value of 3.0 to all units with ten or more members. Each unit's equivalent income was then calculated by dividing its measured income by the appropriate equivalence factor.

The empirical results present data on both equivalent and unadjusted measured income so that the impact of this procedure can be examined.

The weighting of income units

Since income units are of different sizes, it is not obvious that they should be counted equally when measuring income inequality or dispersion, although this has been the conventional practice. As Danziger and Taussig point out:

> The pooling of income by family members, however, does not mean that each family unit should be given equal weight in the construction of the size distribution. In fact, conventional size distributions that weight each family equally violate the requirements for individualistic social welfare functions because they implicitly weight the welfare of an individual inversely to the size of the unit in which he or she lives (1979, p. 366).

In considering this issue, Atkinson suggests that combining the chores of how to value unit income and how to weight the units allows nine different presentational and inequality-measuring procedures:

> Suppose that the income of a family (or household) is Y and that the family has n members. Then we could treat the family as 1 unit with income Y, . . . or as 1 unit with income (Y/n), or with income (Y/n^*), where n^* is the 'equivalent' number of adults. On the other hand, we could treat the family as n units, each with income Y, or each with income (y/n), or each with income (Y/n^*). Finally, we could treat the family as n^* units, with again three possible measures of income (1983, p. 52).

Danziger and Taussig (1979) demonstrated that the choice among the possible procedures is important for the image of inequality which emerges from the data, both cross-sectionally and over time. Which should be used?

Of the nine possibilities in Atkinson's example, there seems little point in considering the final three – those treating the family as n^* units – since this appears to suggest that the importance of an individual's economic welfare is a function of the equivalence scale value of the unit in which he or she resides, and thus is subject to a version of the weakness which Danziger and Taussig's criticism identifies in conventional data. Equivalent adults do not exist, unlike families or individuals, although a family or individual may have an equivalent income. If the family is to be treated as one unit, measuring the distribution of Y/n, or of Y/n^* (each a variation on individual income), tells one something about the economic differences between families, but begs the question of the number of people affected by those differences.[3] If the family is treated as n units, there is no real basis for assuming that each has an income of Y, since this measures neither the income nor the standard of living available to each of them.[4]

This would appear to leave three formulations – family income among families, per capita income among persons and equivalent income among persons – but despite its complexity and apparent comprehensiveness, Atkinson's formulation requires one further element if it is fully to represent the choice of measures available in assessing income dispersion – the method whereby income units are rank ordered.[5]

The rank order of income units

In Atkinson's formulation, the nine possible procedures represent the result of a 3×3 matrix, with three options for unit weight (1, n and n^*) and three for income measure (y, y/n, y/n^*). Once the rank-ordering issue is separately identified, the matrix expands to $3 \times 3 \times 3$, with three options for each of *weight*, *measure* and *rank ordering* (y, y/n, y/n^*).[6] For example, returning to the nine-procedure example used by Atkinson, the additional role of the rank order of units may be illustrated with the cases where the family is treated as n units, with income being either Y or Y/n. One formulation would presumably rank the units by Y, a second by Y/n; but a third procedure could rank the units by Y while measuring, effectively, Y/n when calculating inequality. This third formulation measures the share of total income going to each quintile of persons in the distribution, the persons being ranked by their family income. This would be equivalent to regarding the bottom 20 per cent of the distribution as those 20 per cent of persons living in the units with the lowest incomes. If economic status is commonly perceived in terms of family income, which is the rank ordering implicit in conventional measures of income inequality, then this formulation is at least as appropriate as the measure of the distribution of family income among family units, which is the most commonly used measure of income inequality.

The inclusion of rank order as a specific additional aspect to be considered is approaching the measurement of income inequality does not in practice lead to the replacement of Atkinson's 3 × 3 matrix of procedures with an even more complex 3 × 3 × 3 matrix: just as some of the apparent possibilities in the 3 × 3 formulation have no real claim to being used, so the choice of rank order will often follow logically from the other choices made. This is most clearly so in the case of measuring the inequality of equivalent income: since equivalent income is intended as a measure of the standard of living available to each individual, it is most appropriately used when each individual is weighted equally (n units), with an income valued at Y/n^*, and ranked by Y/n^*. But while the choices may often be aligned, the conceptual difference can be important, as the example in the previous paragraph suggests.[7]

The discussion therefore suggests the use of three measures of income inequality: the measure of equivalent income just outlined and two measures of unadjusted income – the distribution of family income among families, and its distribution among persons ranked by family income. The first of these two unadjusted measures allows comparability with previous studies, both among and within countries, whilst the second is an equally valid measure of the inequality of unadjusted income and services as a useful corrective to the first; since there is no unique truth in these data, it would be inappropriate, however tempting, to argue that the truth may lie in-between these two measures.

A further issue of methodology emerges when the question of the rank of order of income units is considered. It concerns the level or stage of income from which the rank order should be established – if indeed it should remain fixed through the various stages of analysis. One effect of successive additions to income (e.g. from cash transfers) or of taxes may be to change the rank order of income units, regardless of any of the adjustments discussed in the previous paragraph. The dimensions of measured inequality may therefore differ with the measure or stage of income which is used to establish the rank order. This means that empirical analysis can either rerank the data at each stage of income, or can establish one income stage as the primary ranking stage. Rather than choosing one or other of these procedures, however, it may be argued that each is appropriate for different purposes.

If the intention is to examine and compare the degrees of dispersion in any two distributions, then reranked distributions are preferable: the inequality of the distribution of, for example, net income is most accurately portrayed when the units are ranked by net income, and the use of other rank orders will misrepresent the inequality of net income. If, however, the intention is to examine the effect of particular policies or income sources on the income share of a specific group or quantile (such as the lowest quintile of pre-transfer income), or to examine the socio-economic, demographic or income characteristics of specific groups or parts of the distribution, then a predetermined rank order may be required. In the former case, the choice of this rank order will be a function of the purpose or focus of the policy evaluation, but for any examination of the characteristics of particular parts of the distribution, gross income seems the best income stage by which to rank units. This is partly because of the counterfactual weaknesses of other income measures, as discussed earlier, but also because gross income is the closest to being a measure of comprehensive income, and, as such, is the most appropriate choice for a determinate ranking concept.

Since the LIS database allows both reranking and determinate ranking, the empirical analyses presented in this chapter therefore generally rerank data when measuring inequality, but use data ranked by gross income for other aspects of analysis, such as examining the characteristics of the different parts of the distribution. The effects of reranking, both by using equivalence scales and by using different income concepts are also examined.

LIS EMPIRICAL ANALYSIS OF INCOME DISTRIBUTION

Table 2.1 gives information on the relative importance of the income sources, taxes and benefits in each country, as represented in the relevant survey.[8]

The data show wages and salaries accounting for around three-quarters of gross income in Canada and the United States, and less than two-thirds in Israel, Sweden and West Germany, with Norway and the United Kingdom in-between at about 70 per cent. For West Germany and Israel this low figure is balanced

Table 2.1 The relative importance of the income sources, taxes and benefits

Variable	*Average value of variable as percentage of average gross income*						
	Canada	United States	United Kingdom	West Germany	Sweden	Norway	Israel
Wages and salaries	75.7	75.8	72.0	63.1	64.5	69.9	66.1
Self-employment income	5.4	6.7	4.5	16.7	3.7	11.1	16.8
Property income	7.2	5.8	2.7	1.1	2.7	2.7	4.4
Factor income	88.3	88.3	79.3	80.9	70.8	83.7	87.3
Occupational pensions	1.8	2.6	2.5	2.3	0.0[1]	1.2	3.4
Market incomes	90.1	90.8	81.7	83.3	70.8	84.9	90.6

Child benefits	0.9	2.2	1.4	1.3	1.2	2.7
Means-tested benefits	1.4	2.1	0.6	4.4	0.3	0.4
Other cash benefits	6.7	12.9	14.5	23.6	12.7	5.3
Total cash benefits	8.0	17.2	16.5	29.2	14.1	8.3
Private transfers	0.6	1.0	0.2	0.0	0.8	1.0
Other cash income	0.6	0.1	0.0	0.0	0.1	0.0
Gross income	100	100	100	100	100	100
Income tax	16.5	13.6	14.8	28.5	19.1	23.4
Payroll tax (employees)	4.5	3.3	7.7	1.2	6.2	5.3
Net cash income	79.0	83.1	77.5	70.2	74.7	71.3

1. The zero figure for occupational pensions in Sweden is in fact a creation of the data-collection process, since such pensions do exist there but are treated as part of pensions in the cash transfer section of the data.
2. The zero figure for payroll taxes in Canada is a result of their absence from the Canadian data tape; such taxes do exist there, varying in rates from province to province, but they are not included in the results in this paper.

by very high levels of self-employment income – amounting to one-sixth of gross income in each, or more than twice as much as anywhere else except Norway. Earned income therefore accounts for more than 80 per cent of gross income everywhere except the United Kingdom (76.5 per cent) and Sweden (68.2 per cent), the two countries with the lowest shares of self-employment income.

Unusually high levels of property income in Canada and the United States, and above-average levels in Israel, help push these countries towards 90 per cent in the share of gross income accounted for by factor income, with the United Kingdom and West Germany around 80 per cent, and Sweden only just over 70 per cent. When occupational or job-derived pensions are included to arrive at market income, Canada, the United States and Israel all move over 90 per cent.

The data at this point seem already to have divided the countries into three groups:

1. Canada, the United States and Israel, with a very large role for market income, and transfers accounting for less than 10 per cent of gross income.
2. Sweden, with a much smaller role for market incomes, and transfers worth over 30 per cent of gross income.
3. The more mixed group, Norway, West Germany and the United Kingdom, where transfers amount to between 15 per cent and 20 per cent of gross income.

The major element of cash benefits, other cash benefits, not surprisingly follows this pattern. What may be a little more unexpected is the large role of income-conditioned or means-tested benefits in Sweden. At 4.4 per cent of gross income, they are more than twice the proportion in the United Kingdom, the country where they are next most important and where cash benefits as a whole are also second only to Sweden in relative importance. However, the relative role of means-tested cash benefits within the income support system – their share of total transfers – is similar in Sweden, the United Kingdom, the United States and Canada.

After those transfer data, it is not surprising that Sweden also has the highest tax take, with income tax alone averaging 28.5 per cent of gross income. While Israel's income tax is a little less onerous (at 23.4 per cent), a heavier reliance on employee social insurance contributions brings its total direct tax take to very near the Swedish 30 per cent level. Norway and West Germany take about a quarter, and the United States 20 per cent, while Canada and the United Kingdom take around one-sixth.[9]

The sum of cash benefits and direct taxes as a proportion of gross income is a simple indication of the magnitude of the amount of income on which government transfer and tax policies may directly impact, and therefore of the total scope which a government currently has for changing the degree of inequality in the distribution of net cash as compared to market income. Here again Sweden stands apart: its 'impact potential' is almost 60, or twice the US figure. West Germany, Norway and Israel are the higher of the in-between group, at about 40, while Canada and the United Kingdom are around 35.

What effects, if any, do these ranges of differences have?

Comparative income inequality

Table 2.2 contains data on the distribution of gross and net cash income to quintiles of families, and of gross and net equivalent income to quintiles of persons, with Gini coefficients provided for each distribution.

The distribution of gross and net income among families is deficient as a measure of the distribution of economic welfare, but represents a conventional presentation of income inequality data, and allows these results to be compared to Sawyer's, since these gross and net concepts are similar to his pre- and post-tax income concepts. When the distribution of gross income among families is examined, the countries divide into three groups:

1. Those with the highest degree of inequality: the United States, West Germany and Israel.
2. A less unequal group consisting of Canada, the United Kingdom and Norway.
3. Sweden, which seems significantly more equal.

Sweden has the lowest Gini coefficient, almost 3 percentage points lower than the next smallest (Norway), and 10 points below the highest, West Germany. It has the largest bottom quintile share, 6.6 per cent (more than a third higher than

Table 2.2 The distribution of income

Variable	Canada	United States	United Kingdom	West Germany	Sweden	Norway	Israel
							Quintile shares (per cent) of income
Distribution of family gross income among quintiles of families							
Lowest quintile	4.6	3.8	4.9	4.4	6.6	4.9	4.5
Second quintile	11.0	9.8	10.9	10.2	12.3	11.4	10.5
Third quintile	17.7	16.6	18.2	15.9	17.2	18.4	16.5
Fourth quintile	25.3	25.3	25.3	22.6	25.0	25.5	24.9
Top quintile	41.4	44.5	40.8	46.9	38.9	39.8	43.6
Gini coefficient (%)	37.4	41.2	36.5	42.9	32.9	35.6	39.5
Revised West German gini				41.4			
Distribution of family net income among quintiles of families							
Lowest quintile	5.3	4.5	5.8	5.0	8.0	6.3	6.0
Second quintile	11.8	11.2	11.5	11.5	13.2	12.8	12.1
Third quintile	18.1	17.7	18.2	15.9	17.4	18.9	17.9
Fourth quintile	24.6	25.6	25.0	21.8	24.5	25.3	24.5
Top quintile	39.7	41.0	39.5	45.8	36.9	36.7	39.5
Gini coefficient	34.8	37.0	34.3	40.9	29.2	31.1	33.8
Revised West German gini				38.9			

Distribution of family equivalent gross income among quintiles of persons

Lowest quintile	6.7	5.1	7.2	7.9	9.4	8.1	6.1
Second quintile	12.6	11.4	13.0	12.1	14.6	13.6	10.3
Third quintile	17.5	17.1	17.9	16.0	18.5	17.9	15.9
Fourth quintile	24.0	24.2	23.7	21.3	23.3	23.4	23.7
Top quintile	39.2	42.1	37.5	43.4	34.2	37.0	44.0
Gini coefficient (%)	32.7	37.1	29.7	36.3	24.9	28.9	38.2
Revised West German gini				35.2			

Distribution of family equivalent net income among quintiles of persons

Lowest quintile	7.6	6.1	9.0	7.5	10.6	9.9	7.5
Second quintile	13.3	12.8	13.5	12.7	16.1	14.8	11.7
Third quintile	17.9	18.1	18.0	16.1	19.1	18.4	16.8
Fourth quintile	23.8	24.4	23.4	20.7	23.1	22.9	23.7
Top quintile	37.4	38.6	36.1	43.0	31.1	34.1	40.3
Gini coefficient	29.9	32.6	27.3	35.5	20.5	24.3	33.3
Revised West German gini				34.0			

1. The top half of the table weights each family unit equally, whilst the bottom half weights each individual equally; income units are ranked by family gross income in the top part, by family net income in the second part, by gross equivalent income in the third part and by net equivalent income in the bottom part.
2. The West German data are affected by a relatively large number of zero and negative incomes in the sample; the revised Gini excludes income units with such incomes. Revised quintile shares for the data are not yet available.

Norway, and three-quarters as large again as in the United States), the largest second quintile share and the lowest income share in the top quintile, 38.9 per cent – though this is closer to the top quintile in other countries.

The central group of countries, Norway, the United Kingdom and Canada, are clearly less equal than Sweden, but more equal than the remaining three, Israel, the United States and West Germany, on the three criteria which are obvious in the table – the Gini coefficient, and the bottom and top quintile shares. Within this group, Norway has the lowest Gini coefficient and the lowest top quintile share, and a bottom quintile share higher than in Canada and equal to that in the United Kingdom. In turn, the United Kingdom has both a lower Gini and a lower top quintile share than Canada.

Within the group of least equal countries, the rankings are not so clearly defined. Even with a Gini coefficient revised downwards by the exclusion of the high number of zero and negative incomes, West Germany still has a higher Gini than the United States, which in turn is higher than Israel, and the same rank order describes the income shares of the top quintiles. In the bottom quintile, however, the United States has a significantly lower share than either Israel or West Germany, both of whom register bottom quintile shares closer to those of the middle group of countries.

Using these three measures (Gini, and bottom and top quintile shares), therefore, the data on the distribution of gross incomes among families suggest an almost totally determined rank ordering of inequality: Sweden as the most equal, followed by Norway, the United Kingdom, Canada and Israel, with the United States and West Germany ranking as most unequal on different measures.[10]

How do these numbers and rankings compare to those emerging from Sawyer's study, which included all these countries except Israel? Since the data relate to a period about 10 years later than Sawyer's, it is not possible to say that any differences solely reflect the more refined procedures used here – the 'real' distributions in the various countries may have changed also – but the contrast is none the less of interest in 'updating' the impression generated by Sawyer's data.

The main differences in ranking relate to the United Kingdom and to West Germany. In Sawyer's analysis the United Kingdom appeared to be as equal as Sweden, and clearly more so than Norway, whilst the LIS data suggest it is significantly less equal than Sweden, and a little less so than Norway.[11] Sawyer's data also showed West Germany to be more equal than the United States on a range of summary measures, and to have a relatively higher bottom quintile income share than the LIS data show,[12] but they also showed West Germany to have the highest top quintile share of any of the six countries, which is consistent with the picture emerging here. Canada's relative position is the same in both sets of data, but in respect of the actual quintile shares, it appears to be a little more equal in the LIS data, as is also the case with Sweden, while the United Kingdom seems more unequal. The data for the United States, Norway and West Germany (apart from its bottom quintile) are very similar in both studies.

When the gross and net income data in Table 2.2 are compared, the countries divide into two rather disparate groups: direct taxes seem to have relatively large effects on inequality in two of the already more equal countries, Norway and Sweden, and two of the least equal, Israel and the United States, whilst they have smaller effects in Canada, the United Kingdom and West Germany.[13] After direct taxes are taken into account, the income share of the bottom quintile rises by around 1.5 percentage points in Sweden, Norway and Israel – a rise of one-fifth in Sweden, over a quarter in Norway and one-third in Israel. In the other four countries the rises are between 0.5 and 1 percentage point, relative rises of around one-sixth.

Direct taxes also bring about large reductions in the top quintile share in Israel and Norway, reductions of 4 and 3 percentage points respectively, with a 2 point drop in Sweden, but they also have a large effect in the United States, where the top quintile's share falls by 3.5 points. In the other three countries the falls are between 1 and 2 points. The changes in the Gini follow the top quintile shares, with a drop of almost 6 points in Israel, over 4 points in Norway and the United States, and a little under 4 points in Sweden; the falls are beween 2 and 2.5 points in Canada, the United Kingdom and West Germany. Direct taxes therefore reduced relative inequality, on the Gini measure, by more than 10 per cent in Israel, Norway, Sweden and the United States.

If the net income data are now used not to examine the impact of taxation by comparison with the gross distribution, but to look at the picture of net income inequality, a somewhat different pattern and a different rank order emerge from that generated by the gross income distribution. Norway now moves closer to the Swedish image of a distinctively egalitarian society, creating a Scandinavian pair of most equal countries. Israel leaves the group of least equal countries, and becomes the most equal of the middle group, with the United Kingdom and Canada following (in that order). West Germany and the United States continue to make up the least equal group, with West Germany having a higher Gini and a larger top quintile share – but also a larger bottom quintile share.

When the net income data are contrasted with Sawyer's post-tax data, the contrasts are generally similar to those described above in respect of the pre-tax data: the United Kingdom appears less equal, the Canadian data now suggest more equality and the Norwegian data are relatively unchanged. Two differences do stand out, however.

First, the LIS data show a larger equalising tax impact in the United States: the shares of the second and third quintiles increase by more, and that of the top quintile falls by significantly more than in Sawyer's data.[14] Secondly, whereas the gross income data showed higher shares in the bottom two quintiles in Sweden and a lower top quintile share than Sawyer's pre-tax data, the net income data show a higher bottom quintile share – but at the expense of the middle quintile. If the difference between Sawyer's data and the LIS data actually reflects changes over time in the Swedish distribution, these results would imply that the decline in the gross income share of the top quintile has not been accompanied by any drop in their net income position, whilst, however, the stability of the gross income share of the middle quintile conceals a drop in this group's net position.

The distribution of equivalent income

How well do these conventional measures, shares and rankings reflect the patterns of the distribution of economic welfare which the lower part of Table 2.2, focusing on the distribution of equivalent income among persons, seeks to measure?

The effect on relative income shares of transforming the data to equivalent income is varied across countries.[15] In Norway, West Germany and the United Kingdom, the gross income shares of the bottom quintiles rise by almost two-thirds, although those of the top quintiles are less affected. In each case the Gini coefficients drop by almost 7 percentage points, a drop of almost a quarter in measured inequality. In Sweden, the bottom quintile gains by a similar absolute amount (almost 3 percentage points), and although its greater unadjusted share makes this a smaller relative gain, the effect of using equivalent income produces a larger fall (both absolutely and relatively) in the share of the top quintile in Sweden than in any other country. Its Gini coefficient therefore falls by 8 points, so that it too has a drop of a quarter in measured inequality when gross income is transformed by the use of equivalence scales.

In Canada, the United States and Israel the effects on the bottom quintile are less marked, and again there are only slight falls in quintile shares at the top of the distribution in Canada and the United States. In Israel, the top quintile actually has a larger share of both gross and net equivalent income than of the corresponding unadjusted concepts, and its Gini coefficient is only slightly lower on the equivalent than the conventional data.

The equivalencing transformation generally has the same effects on countries at the net as at the gross income levels, but since these data are the best available measure of the inequality of economic welfare in each of these countries, they merit a brief summary. The most notable aspect of the data is the strikingly low degree of inequality in Sweden: the Gini coefficient for the distribution of equivalent net income is only 20.5, and the quintile shares of 10.6 per cent at the bottom and 31.1 per cent at the top are unusually close. In Norway, the second most equal country on these measures, the bottom quintile has just under 10 per cent of net income, whilst in the United Kingdom it has 9 per cent. The average equivalent income of the top quintile therefore exceeds that of the bottom by less than a factor of 3 in Sweden, rising to 3.5 in Norway, 4 in the United Kingdom, 5 in Canada, 5.5 in Israel, almost 6 in West Germany and more than 6 in the United States.

The equivalent income data therefore repeat the rank ordering of inequality suggested by the unadjusted gross income data, though with clearer gaps between the cardinal positions of some of the countries. Sweden is clearly most equal, followed by Norway, the United Kingdom and Canada. Thereafter, the order depends on the measure used: while Israel seems marginally more equal than West Germany at the equivalent net income stage, the United States has the lowest bottom quintile shares, but also has lower top quintile shares than either West Germany or Israel, and thus a lower net income Gini coefficient.[16]

The two adjustments to the gross income data in Table 2.2 – allowing for taxes and transforming for equivalent income – produce different effects in different countries. Sweden and Norway become even more equal as a result of both changes, taxes have a significant effect on the Israeli and the US data, whilst equivalencing has a major impact on the West German and the UK data. Only in Canada does neither have major effects, although their joint effect is important. Such divergences bedevil conventional attempts at comparative inequality analysis, but illustrate a major advantage of the LIS database – that it allows these various measures to be specified and tested, and their different effects examined.

Sources of inequality

In order to explore the proximate reasons and explanations for the patterns of inequality in each country, this section examines the role of a range of income sources in the composition of the gross income of each quintile. For this purpose it is appropriate to use data with a determinate income ranking scheme; data ranked by household gross income, but with each individual weighted equally, are used.[17] Both as a preliminary to the examination of these detailed data, and as the third perspective on measuring inequality which was discussed earlier, the distribution of unadjusted income over quintiles of persons is first examined.

Table 2.3 sets out the quintile shares of factor, gross income and net income in this determinately ranked distribution. In general, the shares of gross income follow the pattern already noted, though with a lesser degree of measured inequality.

Table 2.3 The distribution of income among persons

Income shares (per cent) of quintiles of persons ranked by family gross income

Variable	Canada	United States	United Kingdom	West Germany	Sweden	Norway	Israel
Distribution of factor income among quintiles of persons							
Lowest quintile	5.4	4.2	4.0	2.3	6.5	4.4	4.9
Second quintile	14.9	12.8	15.0	13.8	18.5	17.0	11.6
Third quintile	19.2	19.2	19.9	17.1	18.8	19.6	16.0
Fourth quintile	24.5	25.1	24.9	22.0	23.0	24.2	24.3
Top quintile	36.0	38.8	36.3	44.7	33.2	34.9	43.2
Distribution of gross income among quintiles of persons							
Lowest quintile	9.5	7.5	10.9	10.7	13.7	12.0	9.3
Second quintile	15.6	14.3	15.6	14.7	20.5	17.8	12.5
Third quintile	18.7	18.8	18.7	16.2	18.6	18.4	15.8
Fourth quintile	23.0	23.6	22.9	20.1	20.1	21.6	22.7
Top quintile	33.2	35.9	31.9	38.2	27.1	30.3	39.8
Distribution of net income among quintiles of persons							
Lowest quintile	10.8	9.0	12.4	13.1	16.4	14.7	12.0
Second quintile	16.4	15.9	15.9	15.3	21.2	18.6	14.1
Third quintile	18.8	19.5	18.6	16.0	18.3	18.6	16.8
Fourth quintile	22.6	23.6	22.4	19.3	19.9	21.0	22.1
Top quintile	31.4	32.0	30.6	36.2	24.2	27.2	35.0

1. Each part of the table weights each individual equally; individuals are ranked by family gross income in each part.
2. The West German data are affected by a relatively large number of zero and negative incomes in the sample.
3. Gini coefficients cannot be calculated for these data, since the income unit (the family) is not congruent with the unit weight (the individual).

However, the bottom quintile share in West Germany comfortably exceeds that in Canada or Israel, and almost equals the bottom quintile share in the United Kingdom, so that the country rank orderings of inequality would be a little less clear on this measure. This West German gross income share is more than four times as large as the factor income share of these individuals, a much greater increase (albeit from a much lower base) than in other countries.

In the countries where gross income is most equally distributed, Sweden, Norway and the United Kingdom, the gross income share is more than double the factor share of the bottom quintile, whereas in the United States, Canada and Israel, the factor income share is more than half the gross share. In fact, as the data show, the Canadian and Israeli bottom quintile factor shares are greater than those in Norway or the United Kingdom, and the United States' factor share is also greater than that in the United Kingdom. This highlights the importance of transfer incomes in distinguishing the more equal from the less equal countries (a topic which is explored fully in the discussion of Table 2.4 below).

The distribution of gross income in Sweden, as represented in Table 2.3, also highlights an unusual statistical consequence of Sweden's family structures and relative egalitarianism – that family gross incomes increase less rapidly than family size in the middle of distribution. While it is a characteristic of income distribution data that family size and family income are positively correlated, the average value of the latter usually increases faster. This is not the case in Sweden, with the result that the income share of the middle quintile of persons is lower than that of the second quintile.

Table 2.3 also demonstrates a relatively greater than previously noted degree of equality in the shares of net income among non-reranked persons: only in the United States is the bottom quintile share under 10 per cent, and only in West Germany and Israel is the top quintile share significantly above 30 per cent. The Swedish data are, however, the most notable in this part of the table: they show a ratio of less than 1.5 : 1 in the shares of the top and bottom quintiles – 24.2 per cent compared to 16.4 per cent – and they also show that the effect of taxes further increases the reversal of the relative average position of quintiles, with the second quintile now having a larger share of net income than either the third or the fourth. Whilst this result would vanish if the data were reranked by net income, it focuses attention on the extent to which the Swedish tax system causes income status switching. (Table 2.6 returns to this issue.)

Table 2.4 breaks down gross income by both source and quintile in order to examine the composition of each quintile share, relative both to other quintiles in the same country and to similar quintiles in other countries. Each data item in the table indicates the percentage of total gross income which goes to each quintile in a particular form or type of income.

When the first quintile in each country is examined, an immediate difference is the proportion of gross income going to each in the form of wages and salaries. The Israeli and US figures of around 3 per cent are exceeded only by Sweden and Canada, and are significantly greater than those for the United Kingdom or West Germany. Although each of self-employment income, property income and occupational pensions are quite small at this stage, when they are added to wages and salaries (to form 'market income'), Canada and Israel emerge as the only two countries where more than 5 per cent of gross income goes to the bottom quintile in the form of market income.

It is, however, the share of total gross income going to the bottom quintile as cash benefits which best predicts and determines the overall degree of inequality. With the exception of the West German data, the bottom quintile cash benefit share correlates with the overall judgements on inequality made earlier in this chapter: 9.1 per cent in Sweden, 7.6 per cent in Norway, 6.7 per cent in the United Kingdom, 4.2 per cent in Canada, 3.4 per cent in Israel and 3.2 per cent in the United States. The 8.3 per cent share recorded in West Germany is out of line in terms of the overall pattern of inequality, but is consistent with the high share of gross income going to the bottom quintile in that country; as noted earlier, the source of the high degree of total inequality in West Germany is at the top rather than the bottom of the income distribution.

The main determinant of the quintile shares, and of the rank order of countries, in the three middle quintiles is wage and salary income; other sources of income explain deviations from this pattern, rather than create patterns of their own. In the

Table 2.4 The quintile and income source composition of gross income

Variable	Canada	United States	United Kingdom	West Germany	Sweden	Norway	Israel
				Element as a percentage of total gross income			
Quintile 1							
Wages and salaries	3.6	3.0	2.4	1.5	3.6	2.9	3.1
Self-employment income	0.4	0.2	0.3	0.3	0.4	0.3	0.7
Property income	0.8	0.5	0.5	0.2	0.6	0.5	0.4
Occupational pensions	0.4	0.3	0.8	0.5	0.0	0.4	1.1
Total cash benefits	4.2	3.2	6.7	8.3	9.1	7.6	3.4
Gross income	9.5	7.5	10.9	10.7	13.7	12.0	9.3
Quintile 2							
Wages and salaries	11.3	9.7	10.4	10.5	11.7	12.5	8.4
Self-employment income	0.7	0.7	1.0	0.4	0.7	1.2	1.1
Property income	1.1	0.8	0.4	0.2	0.7	0.5	0.6
Occupational pensions	0.4	0.7	0.6	0.5	0.0	0.4	0.7
Total cash benefits	1.9	2.1	2.8	3.1	7.4	2.9	1.5
Gross income	15.6	14.3	15.6	14.7	20.5	17.8	12.5
Quintile 3							
Wages and salaries	15.1	15.2	14.5	12.6	11.7	14.4	11.8

Self-employment income	1.5	1.6	1.0	1.1	0.8	1.0	0.8
Property income	0.6	0.4	0.6	0.1	0.4	0.8	1.1
Occupational pensions	0.5	0.2	0.0	0.4	0.4	0.5	0.3
Total cash benefits	1.2	1.6	5.3	1.8	2.4	1.0	1.2
Gross income	15.8	18.4	18.6	16.2	18.7	18.8	18.7
Quintile 4							
Wages and salaries	16.8	17.7	15.3	16.6	18.4	19.9	19.4
Self-employment income	3.8	2.2	0.7	1.1	0.8	1.3	0.9
Property income	0.6	0.4	0.3	0.1	0.4	1.0	1.3
Occupational pensions	0.4	0.1	0.0	0.6	0.3	0.5	0.3
Total cash benefits	1.0	1.1	3.9	1.7	2.6	0.8	0.9
Gross income	22.7	21.6	20.1	20.1	22.9	23.6	23.0
Quintile 5							
Wages and salaries	25.9	22.4	22.1	21.9	26.3	28.0	26.3
Self-employment income	9.6	5.9	0.9	13.8	1.5	3.5	2.5
Property income	2.2	0.9	0.4	0.5	0.9	2.7	2.9
Occupational pensions	0.7	0.1	0.0	0.4	0.4	0.6	0.4
Total cash benefits	1.2	0.8	3.6	1.6	2.6	0.8	0.8
Gross income	39.8	30.3	27.1	38.2	31.9	35.9	33.2

The quintiles are composed by ranking persons according to the gross income of their family, so that each quintile contains different numbers of families, but equal numbers of persons. The income and benefit shares are based on the family totals in each quintile. Each figure indicates the percentage of total gross income going to a particular quintile via each income source. The gross income figures include private transfers and other cash income which are not shown in the details.

second and third quintiles, the rank order of gross shares follows that of wages and salaries, except that the higher amounts of cash benefit income in Sweden and the United Kingdom give them larger gross shares than would have been predicted from the wage and salary data. In the fourth quintile, cash benefits no longer have such an effect (although they remain larger in Sweden and the United Kingdom than elsewhere, and the only reordering from the wage and salary pattern is caused by the relatively large amount of self-employment income in Israel.

The shares of the top quintiles, and thus an important aspect of total inequality, cannot, however, be understood by examining wages and salaries. The two countries with the largest top quintile shares of gross income, West Germany and Israel, have relatively low top quintile wage and salary shares – West Germany, in fact, has the lowest of these seven countries – but they have exceptionally high self-employment income shares. Almost 14 per cent of total gross income in West Germany, and almost 10 per cent in Israel, is self-employment income which goes to the top quintile. In Table 2.1 it was noted that self-employment income was unusually large in these two countries, but these data show the massive extent to which, particularly in West Germany, this income goes to the top quintile.

It can now be seen that the high degree of income inequality in West Germany (which was also evident for the top quintile in Sawyer's study) is due to the large and very unequal role of self-employment income there. This also explains a part of the greater inequality in Israel, and contributes to the extent to which the Norwegian distribution is less equal than the Swedish: self-employment income is three times more important in Norway, and almost 90 per cent of it goes to the top quintile, compared to less than a quarter in Sweden.

The analyses thus far have focused on measuring the degree of income inequality in various end-state or static situations, and the contributors to those states of inequality. The next sections of the chapter examine a different aspect of income distribution – the extent to which the rank order of individuals, their economic status, changes under different definitions or measures of the distribution.

Equivalence scales and rank order

The earlier analyses showed that the use of equivalent income generally reduces the degree of measured inequality, and has a greater effect on the measurement of inequality at the bottom of the income distribution than at the top. But it is important to note that those data had been reranked once transformed into equivalent form; the apparent change in inequality would have been greater with data where the rank order was unchanged. This indicates that the argument for using equivalence scales is not just that their use tells one more about the true dimensions of economic inequality, but that it provides a more accurate picture of the composition and characteristics of the various parts of the income distribution. This conclusion is consistent with Sawyer's conclusion in respect of using per capita income:

> Although the change observed in moving from a household distribution to a per capita distribution does not yield drastic changes in the decile shares, it does have a substantial impact on the identity of the people in the various deciles (1976, p. 18).

Since perceptions of which groups in society are low or high income, and of the distributive impact and effectiveness of tax and transfer programmes, are more likely to be based on unadjusted than on equivalent data, the differences in these rank orderings may be of considerable importance for the evaluation of policy.[18] In order to investigate the degree of rank order change caused by the use of equivalence scales, Table 2.5 shows the percentage of persons who are in different deciles of the distributions of family gross income (among quintiles of persons) and of equivalent gross income. It indicates a very high degree of movement – only a quarter of individuals are in the same decline on both measures. The percentage who move three or more deciles varies from 11.8 per cent in the United States to a very high 29.2 per cent in Sweden.

The lower half of the table looks at 'stayers' in terms of their original location. A small majority of those originally in deciles 1 and 10 remain in those deciles, but in the middle of the distribution only one-sixth of households do so – and this figure drops as low as 10 per cent in Norway and Sweden. Therefore, while the poor tend to be poor on either measure (and the rich rich), there is considerable movement in the middle income

Table 2.5 The effect of income equivalencing on the rank order of persons in the income distribution

Percentage of persons[1] in different deciles of the distributions of gross income and of equivalent gross income

Variable	Canada	United States	United Kingdom	West Germany	Sweden	Norway	Israel
Up three or more deciles	8.7	6.6	9.2	8.9	13.6	12.9	8.6
Up two deciles	9.1	11.0	8.1	11.6	10.1	7.0	9.2
Up one decile	15.2	15.8	16.5	12.4	17.7	14.1	15.6
In same decile	26.9	28.9	26.2	28.4	20.5	22.2	31.3
Down one decile	22.9	21.6	23.8	19.2	11.7	23.2	17.6
Down two deciles	11.5	10.8	10.4	11.2	10.9	11.6	9.5
Down three or more deciles	5.8	5.2	5.7	8.4	15.6	9.0	8.2
Further data on stayers – those whose decile remains unchanged[2]							
Percentage of stayers in:							
Decile 1	62.7	66.1	65.5	71.7	63.3	60.0	52.9
Deciles 3 to 8	16.6	18.3	15.0	16.7	10.6	10.3	22.9
Decile 10	53.0	55.8	50.7	54.6	47.7	52.6	63.4
Percentage of stayers in:							
Deciles 1 and 10	43.0	42.2	44.3	44.4	54.0	50.7	37.1
Deciles 1, 2, 9 and 10	63.0	62.1	65.6	64.7	69.0	72.2	56.1

1. The data show the percentage of persons whose gross income decile changes when one moves *from* a measure of family income *to* one of equivalent family income.
2. As the data demonstrate, fewer people experience rises than falls – in each country about one-third whilst around two-fifths fall – but there are a greater number of large rises (which in a sense 'make space' for the greater number of smaller falls).

groups in all the countries. Policy arguments, proposals or analyses which discuss distributional impacts in terms of 'raw' income data may therefore have very different, and perhaps perverse, effects on the distribution of economic welfare. These rank order shifts suggest a need for considerable care in designing and targeting policies which affect the distribution of income.

Equity and rank order

As noted earlier, changes in the rank order of an income distribution due to the addition of transfer income or the removal of taxes can be important for determining the importance of a particular choice of a primary ranking concept. They are also important for examining the policy issue about the choice available to a government as to whether its interventions are intended to 'shuffle' the income distribution – that is, to change rank order – or simply to 'compress' it – that is to narrow the extent of inequality without changing the rank order of individual income units. This is the issue which Plotnick refers to as 'horizontal equity'; 'a horizontally equitable distribution is one that preserves the initial rank order of the units' (1984, p. 4).

Plotnick sets out the view that rank preservation is an important aspect of redistribution policy and analysis, going so far as to argue that:

> The degree to which differences in initial well-being should be narrowed is debatable, but once this is resolved, what social purpose would be promoted by reversing ranks during the transformation? None – if the economic game is regarded as a fair process. . . . Unless the socially optimal distribution is one of full equality, those earning more initial well-being should surely have greater final well-being than those earning less. What logic could justify otherwise? Thus, any reversals incidental to the redistributive process would seem to lower social welfare (1984, pp. 4–5).

One need not accept the fairness or appropriateness of any particular initial rank ordering to accept that the issue of rank order changes is an important aspect of the process of income distribution and redistribution, and one unduly neglected in empirical research. But how should well-being be defined and measured in examining rank order changes? Whilst social policy equity can be more properly judged in relation to changes in equivalent income rank orderings, popular perceptions of tax and transfer equity are more likely to be based on actual income. Similarly, if rank preservation is justified on the basis of the 'economic game' being (or being seen as) a 'fair process', then actual incomes are the relevant measure. In these analyses, incomes are therefore examined unadjusted by equivalence factors.

Table 2.6 indicates the rank order changes between factor and net cash income, and between gross and net cash. Apart from its relevance to horizontal equity, the top half of Table 2.6, showing the moves from factor to net cash income, can be thought of as measuring the net effect of direct taxes and cash transfers – the implicit negative income tax schedule of the tax-transfer system. It shows that only between a quarter and a half of persons remain in the same decile, though most of the changes are of one decile. Sweden again stands out as having the most changes, and it is the only country with any significant number of people changing three or more deciles.

One thing which, not surprisingly, emerges from the data is the extent of shifts in the bottom deciles, reflecting the upward movements of retired households in receipt of social security pensions, and their replacement by poorer working households. In Canada, for example, factor decile 2 loses 64 per cent of its members, 36 per cent moving down to replace those leaving the bottom decile, and 28 per cent moving up. In Sweden, factor decile 2 loses 79 per cent of its members, 26 per cent moving down to replace those leaving factor decile 1.

Rank order changes from gross to net cash income capture the effect of direct taxes on the income hierarchy. As might be expected, these effects are smaller – direct taxes tend to compress rather than to shuffle the distribution. Between 50 and 75 per cent of individuals remain in the same decile, with least change in the United States and Canada and, again, most in Sweden. Stayers are never less than 60 per cent of any decile in Canada and, as elsewhere, moves are mainly in the middle deciles. Stayers are never below 70 per cent in the United States, but almost all (99.8 per cent) of those dropping three or more deciles drop from decile 10 – i.e. almost 5 per cent of that decile's membership drop three or more deciles, and about 1 per cent go to the bottom decile. In the United Kingdom and Norway, stayers never drop below 50 per cent in six deciles, and Israel is similar. In Sweden, stayers fall to as low as 36 per cent, and are below 50 per cent in seven deciles. Even in Sweden, however, most changes are of one decile and only 2 per cent of households move more than three deciles.

Although the majority of the changes identified here are of only one decile, the fact that the rank order of between a quarter and a half of individuals is affected to this extent is surprising and merits further investigation. It may, for example, be the case that the changes are related to the deliberate effects of policies on families of different compositions, particularly since the data in Table 2.6 relate to unadjusted rather than to equivalent income.[19]

The overall impression given by the data suggests that Sweden not only has relatively high tax and transfer shares in family income, and higher levels of inequality-reducing redistribution, but also alters the relative positions of a greater proportion of its population during that process of redistribution. It is, therefore, very successful on measures of vertical equity, but fares less well on the narrower interpretations of horizontal equity.

CONCLUSIONS

In concluding this chapter, it seems appropriate to comment both on what the exercise has shown about comparative income distribution and on its implications for the use of a comparative microdataset like the LIS database.

The income distribution results largely speak for themselves by now. They allow one with a considerable degree of confidence to note an overall pattern in the inequality of income and economic welfare, with a rank order in which Sweden is the most equal, followed by Norway, the United Kingdom and Canada, while among the less equal countries Israel is generally more equal than either West Germany or the United States, whose relative inequality depends on which measure is chosen.

But the LIS database also allows a more detailed explanation of these results, noting, for example, the role of cash benefits in increasing equality in Sweden and the United Kingdom, and in aiding the bottom quintile in West Germany; and the important

Table 2.6 The rank order of persons in the income distribution under different concepts of income

Variable	Canada	United States	United Kingdom	West Germany	Sweden	Norway	Israel
			Percentage of persons who change deciles of the distribution				
Moving from factor income to cash income							
Up three or more deciles	1.9	3.6	4.7	6.9	8.6	3.5	3.9
Up two deciles	3.7	4.3	6.0	5.3	9.6	5.0	5.3
Up one decile	14.5	11.5	14.4	13.8	14.9	16.0	15.6
In same decile	52.4	49.6	37.9	35.5	27.7	42.3	43.9
Down one decile	26.5	29.8	29.9	27.1	19.6	28.1	23.8
Down two deciles	1.0	0.8	6.8	9.3	14.5	4.5	4.6
Down three or more deciles	0.1	0.5	0.4	2.1	5.1	0.6	2.9

Moving from gross income to cash income

Up three or more deciles	0.0	0.0	0.2	0.2	0.2	0.2	0.0
Up two deciles	0.4	0.1	1.1	4.4	4.0	1.9	2.7
Up one decile	11.7	11.8	13.6	20.9	23.3	16.9	21.3
In same decile	75.9	78.4	69.2	54.1	49.2	62.4	57.7
Down one decile	11.7	9.1	15.5	15.8	17.9	16.7	12.0
Down two deciles	0.3	0.2	0.4	2.8	3.5	1.5	4.3
Down three or more deciles	0.1	0.5	0.1	1.7	1.9	0.4	2.0

1. The West German data in the upper part of this table are approximate, because the large numbers of persons living in families with no factor income made it impossible to identify a factor income level which separated the first and second quintiles ranked by factor income. The data displayed are in the middle of the range of possible actual values, a range which extends less than 10% (not 10 percentage points) on either side of each value in the table.

2. The relatively larger number of negative net cash incomes in the German data account for about one-third of those dropping by three or more deciles in each part of this table. The 5% of Swedes who drop three or more deciles are drawn fairly evenly from factor deciles 4 to 10; most drop just three or four deciles.

part played by self-employment income in contributing to the high top quintile shares (and thus to the greater inequality) in West Germany and Israel, and in rendering the Norwegian distribution less equal than that of its Scandinavian neighbour. They also point out the unusually high frequency of rank order changes in the economic status of individuals in the Swedish tax and transfer process. In so doing, the results demonstrate the most important point about the database – its actual value for empirical analysis.

The wealth of the database, however, also emphasises two points which, whilst generally true about comparative research, acquire a more visible importance with good data. First, the database means that methodological issues need to be treated both more explicitly and more carefully; the range of approaches to the data is considerable, and provided an unusual array of choice for a researcher. Secondly, the data raise a wide range of questions whose proper interpretation requires the availability of a considerable degree of knowledge and awareness of the institutional features of the various countries. This indicates that it is important to complement an income microdatabase by access to a database focused on aspects of social structure and institutional provision.

NOTES

Helpful comments on earlier drafts of this chapter were received from Sheldon Danziger, Stephen Jenkins, Gail Oja and Edward Wolff, from LIS colleagues, and during presentations at the Institute for Research on Poverty, Madison, Wisconsin, and the Department of Economics, New York University.

1. This is not explicitly stated in Sawyer's paper, but is strongly suggested by a reading of the manner in which other adjustments were made.
2. It would be interesting to separate the factor income received from government programmes in order to examine the factor beneficiaries of social and other public provision. Even this, however, would not capture the benefits of public spending to private sector sub-contractors, nor the cases where private sector providers are paid by individuals who are subsequently reimbursed, in whole or in part, from public funds.

3. O'Higgins (1985a) argues and empirically demonstrates that for the United Kingdom the details of inequality are, in practice, little different whether measured by equivalent income per family or equivalent income per individual. Whilst the argument can be generalised to most conventional patterns of income distribution, little differences within one dataset may be more significant across seven sets, and, since equivalent income per person is conceptually superior, it is preferable to use it where possible.

4. This would be less true in measuring the distribution of wealth, since the control of power, as distinct from consumption possibilities, which wealth conveys is not reduced if it benefits several individuals.

5. This element is usually ignored. Even Danziger and Taussig's sensitive treatment of this issue (1979, especially pp. 369–70) does not separate the income ranking question from the measuring and weighting issues.

6. Thanks are due to Brigitte Buhmann for correcting an error in a draft discussion of this topic.

7. The separate importance of the ranking issue also emerges when the income concept, whereby relative economic status is measured, differs from that used in examining the components of the income distribution. For example, one might measure the distribution of unadjusted income among people ranked by equivalent income in order to investigate which changes in actual incomes would most help those at the bottom of the distribution of equivalent income.

8. For a discussion of the relationship between survey data and the national accounts picture of the income and fiscal structure of a country, and such evidence as is available in respect of the LIS sample countries, see Chapter 1.

9. The figure for Canada is affected by the absence of any data on payroll taxes in the Canadian tape.

10. The major effects of using other summary measures are obvious from the raw data – the more weight given to the interests of the bottom quintile, the greater the extent to which West Germany will be less unequal than the United States.

11. The explanation might of course be that Sweden and Norway have become more equal since the early 1970s. However, the available data indicate that while this appears to have been the case in Sweden (Aberg *et al.*, 1985), the Norwegian distribution remained unchanged over the relevant time period (Ringen, 1982).

12. The difference in bottom quintile shares is partly explained by the West German zero incomes which were discussed in Chapter 1.

13. While this discussion looks only at taxes, it should be noted that their distributional effects can properly be examined only by also examining the distributional impact of the manner in which they are spent.

14. It should be remembered that these US data relate to a period when the 'bracket creep' caused by fiscal drag had left unusually large numbers of Americans facing higher marginal tax rates. Subsequent

(and consequent?) cuts in the federal income tax will have changed this picture, and the enactment of legislation introducing bracket indexation reduces the likelihood of its reappearance.

15. Although the discussion is in terms of the effects of the equivalencing transformation, it should be noted that the data also change the ranking and weighting concepts, since they are based on quintiles of persons. The effects of moving to a quintile of persons measure with adjusted income are shown in Table 2.3.

16. Since the Israeli data exclude rural inhabitants, it seems likely that even this relatively high level of inequality understates the true degree of inequality in Israel. While this may seem surprising in view of the egalitarian image projected by Israel, it is consistent with Kuznets' arguments that countries at earlier stages of economic development will experience higher levels of inequality. The data in Table 2.4 suggest that the proximate causes of this greater inequality are the lower relative importance of cash benefits and the greater role and more unequal distribution of self-employment income.

17. Arguably, the equivalent income data would be the most appropriate focus for such an examination, as they best measure the distribution of economic welfare. However, the effect of the equivalencing transformation of the data means that the impact of the various income sources would be conflated with the impact of applying equivalence scales.

18. The arguments underlying these assertions are set out, with examples, in O'Higgins (1985b).

19. Some of the movement may also be a function of the use of a relativist measure such as deciles, since a small number of large shifts may induce a large number of consequential small 'shakedown' shifts in order to keep the numbers in each decile equal. This may be especially important in relation to the larger number of shifts in the Swedish data, since in a relatively more equal (and hence dense) distribution the number of such consequentialist shifts will necessarily be greater. This feature of the use of rank orders led Plotnick to argue that 'a measure that examines differences in [actual and rank-preserving] well-being . . . is probably superior to one based on rank differences' (1984, p. 5).

3 · INCOME POVERTY IN SEVEN COUNTRIES: Initial Estimates from the LIS Database

Timothy M. Smeeding, Lee Rainwater, Martin Rein, Richard Hauser and Gaston Schaber

INTRODUCTION: POVERTY AND INEQUALITY

Income poverty is a policy concern in all modern industrial countries. Social scientists in each country conduct studies to describe the low income population, to assess their well-being, and to evaluate the effectiveness of policies designed to improve their situation (e.g. Johannson, 1973; Townsend, 1979).

Increasingly, there has been interest in comparing the size and characteristics of the low income population in different countries, with the long range goal of studying the interrelations between national political and economic systems and problems of low income (OECD, 1976; Beckerman, 1979; Hauser and Nouvertne, 1980; European Community, 1981). However, these studies have been hampered by the necessity to work with non-comparable tabulations which the researcher cannot control. An early study directed to the development of comparable microdata on income is Rainwater *et al.* (1985), which reports on the low income population of persons in midlife course (25–54 years of age) in Sweden, the United Kingdom and the United States around 1970. This chapter uses the LIS database to compare the size and composition of the low income population of Sweden, Norway, Canada, Israel, the United Kingdom, West Germany and the USA.[1]

Poverty as defined in this study is 'economic distance' poverty. Equivalent disposable income is calculated for all families, and then, attributing that income to each person in the family, the median equivalent income of all the persons in the sample is established. The poverty line is defined as one half of that median. Such a line is higher than the national poverty line in some countries (for example, the United States) and lower than the lines in other countries (e.g. the existence minimum in Sweden).

However, among those who try to make cross-national comparisons, a poverty line that is about half of the median standard of living has emerged as a convenient standard (Korpi, 1980). Families whose incomes are below this line clearly are far removed from the mainstream level of living of their societies (Rainwater, 1974; Townsend, 1979). (Variations among countries in non-cash social benefits may certainly mean that there is considerable heterogeneity in the well-being of poor persons in different countries but even so such persons will have a markedly more restricted material standard of living, particularly in terms of the resources they actually control.)

The chapter also provides information on the characteristics of persons in the lowest equivalent income quintile since there is considerable interest in the question of variations among countries in who ends up on the bottom of the distribution of economic welfare (older persons, single-parent families, etc.). In addition, the characteristics of the density of the lower part of the income distribution, as manifested in the relationships between the economic distance poverty line, the bottom quintile line and the median, are important guides to the links between inequality and poverty in any country. For example, in a relatively unequal lower half of the distribution of economic welfare, the ratio of the economic distance poverty line to the bottom quintile line will be closer to 1, while the bottom quintile line will be a smaller proportion of the median. Similarly, a more densely packed distribution is more equal.

Table 3.1, which shows the relations of the bottom quintile and economic distance poverty lines and the median, therefore provides a rapid overview of the pattern of poverty and inequality in the lower half of the income distribution in each of these countries. In general it confirms the results detailed in the previous

Table 3.1 Poverty and the density of the income distribution

Country	Ratio of poverty line to bottom quintile line	Ratio of bottom quintile line to median income
United States	0.90	0.56
Israel	0.87	0.58
Sweden	0.66	0.75
United Kingdom	0.79	0.63
Norway	0.70	0.72
Canada	0.80	0.63
West Germany	0.73	0.68

Notes The bottom quintile line is the upper bound of the lowest equivalent quintile of disposable income. The poverty line is defined as one-half of median equivalent disposable income.

chapter, with the United States and Israel having the greatest degree of poverty-creating inequality, followed by Canada and the United Kingdom. The position of West Germany, close to Norway and Sweden, is also consistent with the evidence in the previous chapter that its relatively high level of overall inequality reflects greater inequality in the upper part of the distributions combined with a relatively less unequal lower half.

The data for the Scandinavian countries are particularly notable for a double-egalitarian effect: not only do they have the lowest poverty line to bottom quintile line and the highest bottom quintile to median ratios, but they are the only two countries where the bottom quintile line is closer to the median than is the poverty line to the bottom quintile. In other words, those on the border of the lowest 20 per cent of economic welfare in Sweden and Norway are closer to the median income than they are to the poverty line.

These ratios do not of course capture all aspects of the relationship between poverty and inequality, and in particular they do not give information on the distribution of individuals within the bottom quintile. If such individuals were evenly spread across the various levels in the bottom quintile, then the ratios of the poverty line to the bottom quintile line would be a good indicator of the relative numbers in poverty; when this is not the

Table 3.2 Post-tax and transfer bottom quintile: millions of persons, families and average family size

Country	Population measure	Total	Population group			
			Elderly families	Single-parent families	Two-parent families	Other families
Sweden	Families	0.892	0.312	0.053	0.171	0.356
	Persons	1.636	0.376	0.146	0.716	0.397
	Persons per family	1.83	1.21	2.75	4.19	1.12
United Kingdom	Familes	1.693	0.997	0.119	0.316	0.261
	Persons	3.657	1.421	0.369	1.514	3.53
	Persons per family	2.16	1.43	3.10	4.79	1.35
Israel	Families	0.145	0.057	0.004	0.064	0.020
	Persons	0.612	0.117	0.017	0.439	0.039
	Persons per family	4.22	2.05	4.25	6.86	1.95
United States	Families	16.939	4.677	3.493	3.492	5.276
	Persons	45.534	9.070	12.514	17.057	6.894
	Persons per family	2.69	1.51	3.58	4.88	1.31
Norway	Families	0.360	0.152	0.041	0.081	0.076
	Persons	0.815	0.210	0.133	0.388	0.084
	Persons per family	2.26	1.30	3.24	4.79	1.11
Canada	Families	1.911	0.515	0.242	0.533	0.620
	Persons	4.753	0.743	0.705	2.497	0.808
	Persons per family	2.49	1.44	2.91	4.68	1.30
West Germany	Families	4.621	1.949	0.228	1.294	1.150
	Persons	10.868	2.784	0.648	5.768	1.677
	Persons per family	2.35	1.43	2.84	4.46	1.44
Average	Persons per family	2.57	1.48	3.24	4.95	1.37

1. Bottom quintile is defined as families or persons in families in the lowest equivalent income quintile.
2. Economic distance poverty is defined as families or persons in families with equivalent income below one-half of median family equivalent income.
3. Families are two or more persons living together who are related by blood, marriage or adoption, or single (unrelated) individuals. More than one family may occupy one household.
4. Elderly families are those headed by a person age 65 or older.
5. Single-parent families are non-elderly families with only one natural parent present and children under age 18.
6. Two-parent families are non-elderly families with two natural parents and children under age 18.
7. Other families are mainly non-elderly childless couples and non-elderly single individuals.
8. Totals may not equal sums across rows owing to rounding errors.
9. UK data are actual number of person or family records, not millions of persons.
10. The Israeli figures are for urban populations only.
11. The average is the simple unweighted average of the seven country estimates.

Kingdom have similar ratios of poverty line to the bottom quintile, but, as will be detailed below, the proportion of people below the poverty line in Canada is almost 40 per cent greater than in the United Kingdom.

The next section examines the relative numbers in poverty in each country, the composition of the poor and likelihood of members of different population groups being in poverty. A further section then examines the impact of the cash transfer systems in different countries on poverty ratios and poverty gaps, both in general and for particular groups.

The three groups on which the analysis focuses are the elderly, single-parent families (with children under 18 living in the family) and two-parent families with children under 18 present. These groups are those towards which social policy and social concern are frequently directed. Social pensions, child allowances and legally enforced alimony play a large role in keeping the elderly and single-parent families from poverty. Any evaluation of a case, similar ratios are compatible with different numbers in poverty. Thus, among the LIS countries, Canada and the United country's social policy must deal particularly with its effectiveness in keeping these two groups from poverty. The 'two-parent with child' family's poverty status is determined more by labour market conditions than by social welfare or income transfer policy. Yet it will be seen that our seven countries' social expenditure systems deal quite differently with two-parent families, since programme eligibility rules and benefit levels for child allowances, for means-tested social assistance and for extended unemployment benefits differ widely across countries. The analysis also identifies 'other families', who are expected to show less poverty than the three main groups. The large majority of persons in this group are non-elderly single persons and married couples without children.[2]

POVERTY RATES AND POPULATIONS

Tables 3.2 and 3.3 present the basic estimates of economic distance poverty. A comparison of the bottom quintile figures in Table 3.2 with overall population figures indicates that the average family size in the bottom quintile of persons is virtually identical to that in the population at large. However, different countries and different groups are not uniformly average.

For instance, in Israel almost all types of low income and poor families are larger than average. This is particularly true for two-parent families in Israel with an average size of almost seven persons! In contrast, elderly families are smaller than average in every country except for Israel. This pattern probably reflects the fact that among older families, the oldest (usually single widows) are the lowest income group. In Israel and Norway low income single-parent families with children are larger than average size, but close to average in other countries. Two-parent families are generally larger than average in all countries, especially (as noted above) in Israel. Among the 'other family' group smaller units are more likely to be low income than larger units. In general, single unrelated individuals have lower incomes than couples due to lack of sharing of incomes and resources, thus explaining this pattern.[3]

Turning to the poverty measures (Table 3.3), a similar pattern emerges, but with a few notable differences. As noted above, there are virtually no poor Swedish elderly measured on this

Table 3.3 Post-tax and transfer economic distance poverty: millions of persons, families and average family size

Country	Population measure	Total	Population group Elderly families	Single-parent families	Two-parent families	Other families
Sweden	Families	0.240	0.001	0.016	0.040	0.183
	Persons	0.410	0.002	0.043	0.166	0.200
	Persons per family	1.70	2.00	2.69	4.15	1.09
United Kingdom	Families	0.741	0.387	0.079	0.130	0.145
	Persons	1.606	0.532	2.37	0.751	0.186
	Persons per family	2.17	1.37	3.00	5.01	1.28
Israel	Families	0.109	0.048	0.002	0.645	0.013
	Persons	0.446	0.096	0.009	0.314	0.026
	Persons per family	4.09	2.00	4.50	6.98	2.00
United States	Families	14.289	3.759	3.168	2.774	4.587
	Persons	36.879	5.687	11.479	13.795	5.919
	Persons per family	2.58	1.51	3.62	4.97	1.29
Norway	Families	0.087	0.023	0.015	0.017	0.033
	Persons	0.195	0.030	0.047	0.081	0.037
	Persons per family	2.24	1.30	3.13	4.76	1.12
Canada	Families	1.145	0.193	0.197	0.309	0.446
	Persons	2.882	0.302	0.580	1.442	0.556
	Persons per family	2.52	1.56	2.94	4.67	1.25
West Germany	Families	1.580	0.687	0.129	0.206	0.558
	Persons	3.234	0.980	0.361	1.047	0.842
	Persons per family	2.05	1.43	2.80	5.08	1.51
Average	Persons per family	2.47	1.60	3.24	5.02	1.36

Notes: As for Table 3.2.

basis.[4] Among single- and two-parent families with children, average family size among the poor is about the same regardless of which definition of poor is used, except for two-parent poor families in the United Kingdom and Israel which are a bit larger by the second, more severe poverty definition. In these countries, the poorest among the poor are living in larger families.

Poverty rates

Intercountry differences in poverty rates among persons can be most clearly seen in Table 3.4. The bottom quintile counts the lowest 20 per cent of persons in families ranked by equivalent income in each country. Within each country these low income rates vary widely among groups. For instance, almost half of all persons in the UK elderly families are among those in the bottom quintile. In contrast, only about a quarter of Swedish and US elderly are so situated.

In Israel only between a fifth and a quarter of single-parent families are in the bottom quintile, compared to over half in the USA and over two-fifths in Canada. In general, single-parent families have the highest proportions in the bottom quintile: the average chance of a single-parent family being in the bottom quintile over the entire group is greater than 3 in 8. There is much less variance among two-parent families with between 15 and 22 per cent of this group in the bottom quintile. In all cases low quintile proportions are lowest among the 'other' group, with the relatively high figures in Sweden most likely including college students who are counted as living alone even when living with their parents.[5]

By contrast, economic distance poverty among persons in two-parent families exceeds 10 per cent only in Israel, the United States and Canada. No country has more than 9.8 per cent of other families in poverty. The West Germans have reduced two-parent poverty rates to Scandinavian levels.

INCOME TRANSFERS AND POVERTY

One important dimension of intercountry comparisons of poverty is the ability of the social welfare system – the cash transfer

Table 3.4 Post-tax and transfer poverty rates for persons: bottom quintile and economic distance measures

Country	Measure		Percentage of persons in:			
		Total (%)	Elderly families (%)	Single-parent families (%)	Two-parent families (%)	Other families (%)
Sweden	Bottom quintile	20.0	24.3	31.4	21.5	14.0
	Economic distance	5.0	0.1	9.2	5.0	7.0
United Kingdom	Bottom quintile	20.0	48.3	45.3	15.2	7.7
	Economic distance	8.8	18.1	29.1	6.5	4.1
Israel	Bottom quintile	20.0	28.9	22.3	15.2	8.1
	Economic distance	14.5	23.8	11.8	14.9	5.5
United States	Bottom quintile	20.0	25.4	56.4	15.9	11.4
	Economic distance	16.9	20.5	51.7	12.9	9.8
Norway	Bottom quintile	20.0	31.7	35.3	16.2	13.0
	Economic distance	4.8	4.6	12.6	3.4	5.7
Canada	Bottom quintile	20.0	28.3	45.6	19.1	12.4
	Economic distance	12.1	11.5	37.5	11.0	8.5
West Germany	Bottom quintile	20.0	27.6	32.6	21.6	10.7
	Economic distance	6.0	9.3	18.1	3.9	5.4
Average	Bottom quintile	20.0	30.6	38.4	18.6	11.0
	Economic distance	9.7	12.7	24.3	8.2	6.6

Notes: As for Table 3.2.

system in particular – to prevent persons and families with otherwise inadequate private incomes from falling into poverty. Table 3.5 presents estimates of the percentage of total persons and persons in each group who are poor on the basis of market and equivalent disposable income. The percentage of pre-transfer poor pulled out of poverty is also given.

Overall about a quarter of all persons lie in families with pre-transfer equivalent incomes below half of the median. With the exception of Sweden, this overall ratio varies only from 24.1 per cent in Norway to 29.1 per cent in Israel. The very large Swedish welfare state and our inability to separate occupational from social pensions here (and also to some extent in Norway) contribute to the high overall pre-transfer poverty rate. But otherwise within-group differences are much larger. As mentioned above, some of this problem is purely definitional. Because of the heavy reliance on public sector pension transfers – i.e. social security retirement pensions – among the elderly, pre-transfer poverty rates for this group will be, by definition, very high everywhere except in countries which rely more heavily on occupational pensions (which are counted as pre-transfer income in this study).

In the United States, where occupational pensions play a large role for only a minority of the elderly, we still find 72 per cent are pre-transfer poor. Israel has a relatively young occupational pension system but still has the lowest pre-transfer elderly poverty rates. This may also be attributable to the propensity of the elderly to live with their children and/or the prevalence of regular interhousehold transfers between extended families. Average retirement age also affects this pattern. West Germany has the highest pre-transfer poverty rate among the elderly, but also the lowest age of retirement. Thus most elderly persons (in families headed by a person aged 65 or over) in West Germany have no earnings. In Israel, earnings and property income are much more prevalent among the elderly than in West Germany and in the USA, as indicated in more detail in the following chapters.

Among single-parent families, pre-transfer poverty rates reflect two things; the ability of single mothers to generate their own earned income, and the effectiveness (and generosity) of alimony and child support laws. Countries with high proportions of single parents who are pre-transfer poor – the United Kingdom, the

Table 3.5 Pre- and post-transfer economic distance poverty rates for persons

Country	Poverty	Total (%)	Elderly families (%)	Single-parent families (%)	Two-parent families (%)	Other families (%)
		Percentage of persons who are poor:				
Sweden	Pre-transfer	41.0	98.4	55.0	21.3	30.5
	Post-transfer	5.0	0.1	9.2	5.0	7.0
	Percentage reduction	87.8	99.9	88.3	76.5	77.0
United Kingdom	Pre-transfer	27.9	78.6	56.3	17.6	12.8
	Post-transfer	8.8	18.1	29.1	6.5	4.1
	Percentage reduction	68.5	77.0	48.3	63.1	68.0
Israel	Pre-transfer	29.0	56.8	52.6	26.1	14.3
	Post-transfer	14.5	23.8	11.8	14.9	5.5
	Percentage reduction	50.0	58.1	77.6	42.9	61.5
United States	Pre-transfer	27.3	72.0	58.5	16.0	15.4
	Post-transfer	16.9	20.5	51.7	12.9	9.8
	Percentage reduction	38.1	71.5	11.6	19.4	36.4
Norway	Pre-transfer	24.1	76.9	44.0	7.8	18.7
	Post-transfer	4.8	4.6	12.6	3.4	5.7
	Percentage reduction	80.1	94.0	71.4	56.4	69.5
Canada	Pre-transfer	25.6	73.6	48.4	18.5	15.2
	Post-transfer	12.1	11.5	37.5	11.0	8.5
	Percentage reduction	52.7	84.4	22.5	40.5	44.1
West Germany	Pre-transfer	28.3	80.3	34.8	12.9	20.1
	Post-transfer	6.0	9.3	18.1	3.9	5.4
	Percentage reduction	78.8	88.4	47.1	69.8	73.1

The percentage reduction is measured as (post − pre)/(pre). All other notes are as for Table 3.2.

United States, Canada and Israel (though the latter has very few single-parent units) – reflect low earnings and poor private alimony/child support arrangements. Particularly in large diverse countries with state (United States) or provincial (Canada) child support collection systems, it is often difficult to enforce these laws effectively. The West Germans do the best here (most likely because of their programme to make advance payments to solo parents where the absent parent is behind time in meeting child support obligations), followed by Norway and Canada.

Pre-transfer poverty among two-parent families reflects relatively low wages among earners and/or high unemployment. Israel, Canada, West Germany, the United Kingdom and the United States had high unemployment during their survey years.[6] The West Germans and Norwegians both have high wages at the bottom of the distribution (more so for West Germany) but only the Norwegians had a relatively low unemployment rate (2.0 per cent) in their survey year.[7] Pre-transfer poverty among persons in 'other' families shows less variance than the other sub-groups, except in Sweden where the adult units' income accounting practice may disguise intrafamily income sharing.

The largest differences are, of course, in the ability of the transfer system to pull the pre-transfer poor over the poverty line. The overall variance here runs from over 87.8 per cent of the pre-transfer poor removed from poverty in Sweden to only 38.1 per cent in the United States. Countries with larger transfer systems (as a percentage of gross domestic product, GDP) are more effective in this regard than are countries with smaller transfer systems. Thus the United States and Canada do relatively poorly, while Sweden, Norway, West Germany and the United Kingdom do better. The Israeli situation is less easily explained. However, high inflation rates in Israel coupled with lags in child allowance and old age pension cost of living adjustments keep many families close to, but just below, the poverty line.

Again, however, these overall figures hide considerable intergroup differences. The West German and Canadian public old age pensions systems are second only to those of Norway and Sweden in preventing poverty among the elderly. The UK system is close behind. Some countries, Sweden in particular, but also Norway and Israel, are very effective in pulling pre-transfer single-parent units from poverty. Other countries do a middling job (e.g. the United Kingdom and West Germany), while Canada and the United States in particular do a very poor job.

Among two-parent families, the generosity and availability of unemployment aid, social assistance and/or child allowances determine the effectiveness of the transfer system in preventing poverty. Here the West German and UK systems do the best job, followed by Norway. Less than half of the pre-transfer poor are pulled out of poverty in Israel (42.9 per cent) and Canada (40.9 per cent), owing to very large families in Israel and low benefit rates for these families in Canada (i.e. a universal but quite modest child allowance programme). In the United States, where extended unemployment benefits, child allowances and social assistance (other than Food Stamps) are virtually non-existent, less than 20 per cent of the pre-transfer poor persons in two-parent families are pulled out of poverty. While both Canada and the United States subsidise children through special income tax exemptions and child care deductions, these are not enough to prevent widespread poverty among parents and children in families which experience long-term unemployment or low wages or both.

Poverty gaps

Poverty headcounts often mask the depth of poverty among poor persons, as measured by their poverty gap: the total dollar differential from the poverty line. The pre- and post-transfer poverty gaps in Table 3.6 correspond to the pre- and post-transfer poverty rates shown in Table 3.5. Poverty gaps are defined as the aggregate equivalent income distance from the poverty line as a percentage of the poverty line. Thus pre-transfer poverty gaps exceed post-transfer gaps.

Whereas overall pre-transfer poverty rates in Table 3.5 were quite similar across countries, pre-transfer poverty gaps differ dramatically in some cases. For instance the West German dataset indicates a high degree of pre-transfer income deficit (86.3 per cent of the poverty line), followed by Sweden (80.7 per cent) and by Norway (79.9 per cent). The United Kingdom, the United States and Canada are close together at about 70 per cent while in Israel the pre-transfer poverty gap is only about 57.6 per cent on average. Post-transfer poverty gaps differ by less, but are still

Table 3.6 Pre- and post-transfer poverty gaps: equivalent income deficit as a percentage of poverty line

Country	Economic distance poverty	Total (%)	Elderly families (%)	Single-parent families (%)	Two-parent families (%)	Other families (%)
			Percentage poverty gap among persons living in:			
Sweden	Pre-transfer	80.7	97.8	57.3	39.0	67.4
	Post-transfer	40.0	45.2	33.4	28.2	43.2
	Percentage reduction	50.4	53.8	41.7	27.7	35.9
United Kingdom	Pre-transfer	72.6	83.1	67.1	33.0	70.7
	Post-transfer	16.0	10.9	17.7	10.8	24.3
	Percentage reduction	78.0	86.9	73.7	67.3	65.6
Israel	Pre-transfer	57.6	72.1	55.5	36.6	58.3
	Post-transfer	16.3	13.4	13.7	20.4	13.3
	Percentage reduction	71.7	81.4	75.3	44.3	77.2
United States	Pre-transfer	71.0	81.2	59.3	43.0	67.1
	Post-transfer	39.9	29.1	43.0	33.3	50.6
	Percentage reduction	43.8	64.2	27.5	22.6	24.6
Norway	Pre-transfer	79.7	87.4	59.7	37.1	79.5
	Post-transfer	40.8	48.3	27.7	29.2	47.6
	Percentage reduction	48.8	44.7	53.6	21.2	40.1
Canada	Pre-transfer	69.8	83.3	72.3	42.0	65.7
	Post-transfer	33.9	18.8	37.0	30.5	41.8
	Percentage reduction	51.4	77.4	48.8	27.4	36.3
West Germany	Pre-transfer	86.3	94.1	61.1	36.6	81.4
	Post-transfer	30.6	28.5	31.4	23.2	48.4
	Percentage reduction	68.2	69.7	48.6	36.6	40.5

Notes: As for Table 3.5.

substantial. After transfers, the average Israeli and UK poor family is only 16 per cent away from its poverty line. In Canada the difference is about one-third, and in West Germany about 30 per cent, while in the United States, Sweden and Norway, the remaining post-transfer poverty gaps are about 40 per cent.

The relative ability of transfer systems to reduce poverty gaps is not always the same as their effectiveness in reducing poverty rates. For instance, Sweden and Norway showed the largest reduction in pre-transfer poverty rates in Table 3.5, but the third and second lowest reduction in poverty gaps in Table 3.6.[8] Some part of this difference may be due to the fact that among those few persons left in poverty in the Scandinavian countries, there are persons who are not eligible for assistance or who understate their real incomes. West Germany was second best at reducing pre-transfer poverty rates, but not as effective at reducing the poverty gap as were Israel or the United Kingdom. The US transfer system was worst at reducing both rates and gaps, followed by the Canadians, Israelis and the United Kingdom.

Group-specific differences in poverty gap reductions are also interesting. The Norwegians and Swedes did worst of all among the elderly (though the numbers remaining in poverty in each country were very small – only 4.6 per cent of the elderly remained poor after transfers in Norway and the figure is almost zero in Sweden). In the United Kingdom and in Israel, poverty gap reductions are largest for both the elderly and for single parents. The United States does poorly for single parents as previous evidence would predict; but so do the Swedes relative to other countries. For two-parent units, the British unemployment and child allowance system is most effective in reducing the pre-transfer poverty gap. Israel does second best, even given the substantial fraction of large, poor, two-parent families after transfer.

While Sweden, Norway and Canada do a better job of reducing pre-transfer poverty rates than the United States, the Canadians do not do much better and the Norwegians the worst in reducing the poverty gap for these two-parent units (but see note 8). The United Kingdom and Israeli transfer systems both fill a high fraction of the poverty gap among 'other' poor families. All things considered, the United Kingdom income maintenance system appears to be most effective in reducing poverty gaps, followed by the Israelis. Both are characterised by universal transfer systems that offer high coverage but fairly low benefit rates. Other than the reduction in the poverty gap for persons in two-parent families, the Israelis compare well with the United Kingdom.[9,10]

SUMMARY AND CONCLUSIONS

The findings presented above indicate that the United States has the highest overall poverty rate, with Israel and Canada following. The Scandinavian countries have the lowest poverty rates with West Germany and the United Kingdom in-between.

Poverty among groups differs in many important ways. There are few if any elderly poor in Sweden, but many elderly poor in the United Kingdom. Poverty in single-parent, largely female-headed, families is a major problem in all countries (unless, as in Israel, there just are not very many female heads). Among two-parent families, poor units tend to be large (e.g. Israel) and more prevalent in countries with relatively weak income support systems for intact families (United States), or with relatively low earnings potentials (United Kingdom). Extended periods of unemployment with little public aid plays a large role. The 'other' group is generally a hodge-podge of childless couples or younger single persons with relatively low poverty rates.

The effectiveness of the income transfer system in reducing poverty is strongest in Sweden, Norway and West Germany, and also in the United Kingdom. The largest intercountry differences are noted for two-parent units where absence or presence of child allowances, extended unemployment compensation and means-tested social assistance produce large differences in effects.

The United Kingdom does remarkably well in reducing the pre-transfer post-tax poverty gap given their relatively low percentage of GDP spent on income transfers. Countries with large and well-developed welfare state transfer systems, e.g. West Germany, Norway, Israel and Sweden, tend to do better than those with less well-developed systems (e.g. the United States and Canada).[11]

Homeownership does not affect the ranking of countries by poverty rates, but in all countries except West Germany those with homes have substantially lower poverty rates than those without homes.

The reasons for these results are not always obvious, but can be traced to several proximate causes. First and foremost, expenditure on income transfers as a percentage of GDP help explain the overall effectiveness of the transfer systems in reducing poverty. Secondly, the universality of the transfer system in terms of helping all or only certain types of poor citizens is important. Finally the structure of the pension system and of wages in the private economy are important.

The Scandinavians and West Germans spend higher proportions of GDP on income transfers, between 15 and 20 per cent of GDP, as compared to around 10 per cent in the United Kingdom, the United States and Canada (OECD, 1985). All countries but the United States and Canada have strong and nearly universal income maintenance systems. Only the United States has no child allowance programme (though there is a means-tested near-cash Food Stamp programme). The UK system seems fairly well targeted on the poor as does the Israeli system.

One interesting point is the strong effectiveness of Israel in reducing the poverty gap (71.7 per cent) as compared to its ability to reduce the poverty count (50.0 per cent), and the opposite result in Sweden where the poverty count falls by 80.7 per cent and the poverty gap only by 50.4 per cent. Norway is much the same as Sweden. Israel's strong universal transfer system helps virtually all low income families, but because of indexation lags, transfers do not rise as fast as wages. Thus the gap falls by more than the count. In Sweden and Norway the few poor who are left are far below their poverty lines. This possibly reflects inconsistencies in the definition of income units and/or uncounted income among these persons.

In contrast, the US system is plagued by categorical eligibility rules which provide meagre benefits for some (e.g. two-parent units) and relatively plentiful benefits for others (e.g. the elderly). Both the United States and Canada have large intergovernmental (i.e. interstate and interprovince) differences in benefit levels and problems in child support enforcement mechanisms which help explain the relatively weak anti-poverty effectiveness of their transfer systems.

Low wages in the United Kingdom and wide wage differentials coupled with a weak unemployment benefit system in the United States help explain the higher poverty and lesser anti-poverty effect transfers in these countries. The West Germans and Scandinavians have relatively high wages even at the bottom end of the wage distribution, thus helping keep poverty rates among two-parent and 'other' families fairly low.

For the elderly, those countries with high minimum pension levels, e.g. Sweden, or high universal social assistance minima, e.g. West Germany, have low poverty rates. For countries with less unified systems (United States, Canada) or for countries with relatively low minimum pensions (United Kingdom) poverty rates are higher among the elderly.

The most significant result is the apparent failure of almost all countries to deal adequately with the single-parent family problem. There are no universal social insurance programmes for these specific families in any of our countries. Most receive child allowances, while some countries do better than others in enforcing income support from the absent parent. The overall average poverty rate for this group is 38.4 per cent – going as high as 51.7 per cent in the United States. Even in Sweden almost 10 per cent of persons in these families are poor.

NOTES

We would like to thank the Ford Foundation, the Government of Luxemburg, the Special Collaborative Programme 3 at the University of Frankfurt and Computer Resources Incorporated (CRI) for their support in completing this project. In particular we are indebted to Günther Schmaus for his painstaking work in preparing the tabulations which underlie this paper, to our LIS colleagues (Lea Achdut, Yossi Tamir, Stein Ringen, Peter Hedstrom, Geoffrey Stephenson and especially Michael O'Higgins) and to Gail Oja and Ken Chomitz for their perceptive comments on an earlier draft.

1. The major features of the data, concepts and definitions used in this chapter (except in reference to poverty) are explained in Chapter 1.
2. While several of the country data files allow the identification of the disabled, who often live alone or with a spouse, they are not separately identified in this chapter; most are therefore in the 'other' category.

3. Possibly this is due to a definition of family which ignores income and household capital sharing among unrelated individuals who live together in the same household (or housing unit).

4. On this basis, only one elderly poor two-person family record, with some negative income amounts but with overall positive income, was found in Sweden.

5. In fact, there are 73,000 single persons under age 25 who were primarily students in the bottom quintile of the Swedish distribution. These make up only 4.5 per cent of all persons in the bottom quintile but 18.4 per cent of the 'other' group. It cannot be determined whether these students are truly living alone at low income levels, or whether they are living alone but are economically dependent on other persons (e.g. parents), or whether they actually live with their parents.

6. A large part of Israel's pre-transfer poverty problem is also due to large family size relative to low wages among earners in this situation.

7. All data are for 1979 except for Canada and West Germany, both of which were for 1981. West Germany's overall unemployment rate was 5.3 per cent in 1981. However, much of this unemployment is thought to be concentrated among foreign guest-workers who are largely excluded from this dataset.

8. The Norwegian dataset does not include local social assistance and local extended unemployment benefits. Although these are less than 0.8 per cent of total survey income, they could be a considerable uncounted share of the poverty gap given the low poverty rate of 4.8 per cent in Norway.

9. The equivalence scales used in this study are rather more generous to larger families than are many other equivalences. This means that very large families such as those in Israel find the equivalence factor (which divides into cash income to produce equivalent income) depresses their equivalent incomes considerably. If a different equivalence scale – one that did not allow for such generous increased levels of income for third, fourth or fifth children – were used, Israeli two-parent poverty rates might be considerably lower.

10. All the figures are based on either annual or subannual incomes. There is no account taken of wealth in the form of financial or non-financial assets. Because income from financial assets is usually poorly reported on surveys (e.g. Radner, 1983), poverty among renters and owners was compared in order to get some idea of the permanence of poverty among families, the rationale being that poor renters are more likely to be long-term poor than are poor homeowners. If homeownership is a sign of higher than average net worth and higher long term income, policies should perhaps be more concerned with poverty rates among renter families as opposed to overall family poverty rates. While both the variance and level of poverty rates among renters is higher than the variance and level of poverty rates among the population at large, there is virtually no change in ranking. Countries with high relatively absolute poverty

rates among the whole population also have high rates among renters and vice versa.

11. One must be careful to note that in some well-developed social welfare states, e.g. Sweden and West Germany, high pre-transfer poverty rates may be due to the systems themselves, in that the confidence in publicly channelled income adequacy in old age reduces the need to prepare other sources of old age income (while the necessary tax rates may also reduce the resources available to do so).

4 · AGE AND INCOME IN CONTEMPORARY SOCIETY

Peter Hedstrom and Stein Ringen

THE FLUCTUATION OF ECONOMIC WELL-BEING

In his classic study of poverty in York at the turn of the century, Seebohm Rowntree (1901) found that the economic well-being of families tended to fluctuate over the life course. The typical career of a family had the form of a 'cycle of poverty' whereby families moved in and out of periods of low economic well-being. Rowntree identified two periods in which families faced the highest risk of poverty, the periods of child rearing and of old age.

The economic well-being of a family depends largely on its size and its total income. In Rowntree's time, there was typically one main income earner in the family, the husband, and only minor additional (cash) incomes were brought in by the wife or older children. Until old age, and with the exception of periods of unemployment for the husband, the income of the family usually did not change very much. But since family size varied considerably over the life cycle – there were often many children – the standard of living of the family still fluctuated significantly. During the period of child rearing it was pressed down; as the children grew older and moved out of the parent family, the latter's standard of living increased even if its income remained about the same; and then, in old age, the standard of living usually fell again, but now because of lower earnings and the lack of alternative income sources such as social security.

Since Rowntree's time, many of the factors underlying the poverty cycle have changed. Changes in family size and composition, the increased labour force participation of women, and, above all, the development of the welfare state have affected the general level of economic well-being of families as well as the degree to which this level fluctuates over the life cycle. However, the basic demographic factors underlying Rowntree's cycle are the same, and an important issue in social policy debate is the extent to which welfare programmes counteract or eliminate this cycle. In particular, because of the ageing of the populations of industrial nations, there is a great deal of concern with the economic status of the elderly.

This chapter reports the results of an analysis of the relative economic position of families in various age groups in seven industrial nations around 1980. Its primary purpose is to describe in general terms the distribution of income among age groups in these countries in a comparative framework. Two main questions are addressed. First, is the kind of fluctuation of economic well-being over the life course that Rowntree described almost a century ago still a characteristic of the distribution of income in advanced industrial nations? Do young and old families continue to have a lower standard of living than the rest of the population and, if so, is this equally true in all nations? Second, moving beyond this purely descriptive problem, to what extent can differences between nations in this respect be explained by differences in the relative roles of income transfer policies?[1]

The paper is divided into three sections. The first examines the composition of family income to see how families put together 'packages of income' (Rainwater et al., 1985) from various sources. The second analyses how the level and distribution of income varies between age groups and across nations. The concluding part discusses the possible relationships between different income packages and the level and distribution of income.

INCOME PACKAGES

A useful way of describing the political economy of contemporary society is in terms of different 'claims systems' varying in importance from one country to another (see Rein, 1983). The major systems within which claims are established in industrial societies are the family, the government and the market (work and capital). Individuals make claims on economic resources against each of these institutions. How families put together packages of income from various sources depends on the availability of the various forms of income and the propensity of each family to choose the available income forms. This availability is, in turn, influenced by macro-economic conditions, welfare policies and other factors, and the families' choices by, for instance, their demographic composition and position in the life cycle.

The seven countries included in this study differ both in the availability of various forms of income and in family composition. For example, public spending on income maintenance around 1980 amounted to over 17 per cent of GDP in West Germany compared with around 10 per cent in the United Kingdom and a little less in the USA (OECD, 1985). As can be seen from Table 4.1, these countries also differ from one another in respect of family size and age composition. In terms of average family

Table 4.1 Size and age distribution of families

	Persons per family	Age group		
		< 24	25–64	65+
Canada	2.7	10	73	17
West Germany	2.4	5	66	29
Israel	3.4	3	74	23
Norway	2.5	7	66	27
Sweden	1.9	14	60	26
United Kingdom	2.7	6	68	26
United States	2.6	10	70	20

1. There are some differences in family definition between the data files. Most important, in the Swedish data single persons over 18 years of age are counted as a family of their own even if they in fact belong to another family. This will for example be the case with students who live with their parents. (Cohabitants who are not married are counted as a married couple.) Household size in Sweden therefore is underestimated. The true figure should probably be close to that of West Germany or Norway. This occasionally influences the interpretation of some of the results for Sweden, as is explained in the text.
2. Families are assigned to age groups according to the age of the family head. In families with a married couple, with or without other members, the family head is the husband.

size, Israel and Sweden are polar cases, Israel having on average larger families than the other countries (3.4 members), and Sweden smaller ones (1.9 members). As for age composition, West Germany has the 'oldest' population and Canada and the United States the 'youngest' population. Israel is a case of its own with relatively small groups of both young and old families and consequently a larger proportion of middle age groups.

The age composition of a population is likely to affect the income package in several ways. An increase in the proportion of elderly people, for example, will reduce the role of earnings, and, by affecting the relative numbers of 'supporters' and 'supported', increase the size of the public redistributive system and the relative role of public transfers. Differences between countries in the way families put together income packages are therefore to be expected. Figure 4.1 shows the composition of total gross family income, first for all families taken together and then for families in different age groups. It distinguishes five different income sources: earnings (employment and self-employment income), capital income, public transfers, occupational pensions and a miscellaneous category labelled other income. The diagram replicates the data in Table 2.1, indicating that there are differences between these countries in the composition of family income, and shows how they differ from each other in this respect.

Examining first the general population, it is clear that earnings are by far the most important income source in all countries. They contribute between 83 per cent (Israel) and 68 per cent (Sweden) of the average family's pre-tax income.

The most significant difference between these seven nations concerns public transfers. These contribute between 8 per cent (Israel/USA) and 29 per cent (Sweden) of pre-tax family income. A second major difference is the important role played by capital income in Canada and the United States (and to some extent Israel) as compared with the other countries.

With some risk of oversimplifying, one can distinguish between a typical European and a typical non-European income package, where the latter is characterised by a relatively low level of public transfers and a high level of capital income. Among the European countries, Sweden is a case of its own owing to its exceptionally

AGE AND INCOME IN CONTEMPORARY SOCIETY 81

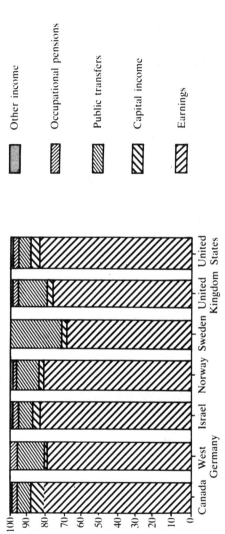

Figure 4.1 Family income packages as a percentage of total gross income. (It has not been possible to distinguish between public transfers and occupational pensions in the Swedish data. However, occupational pensions in Sweden are a minor component, about the same as in Norway.)

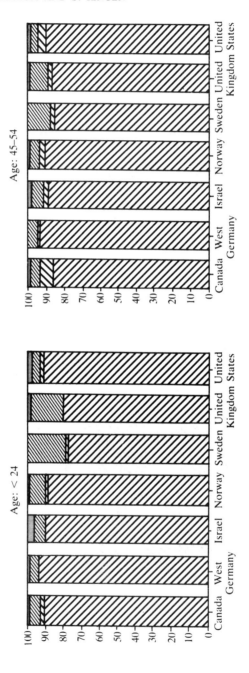

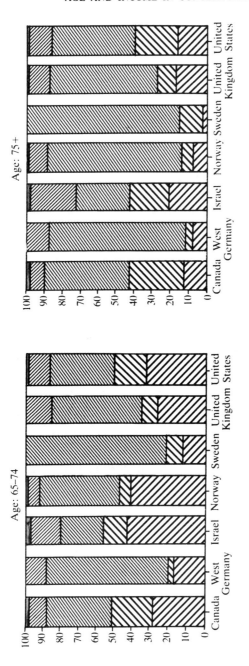

Figure 4.1 continued

high level of public transfers (close to 30 per cent of pre-tax family income).

Are these differences in income package what one would expect to find on the basis of the variations in age composition described above? To some extent, yes. The non-European countries have relatively 'young' populations and it is therefore to be expected that transfer incomes matter relatively less there. But differences in demographic composition do not explain the entire variation. The very significant role played by public transfers in Sweden, for example, cannot be explained by its demographic structure since Sweden does not have an 'older' population than the other European countries. There is reason, therefore, to believe that the high level of public transfers in Sweden is a result of different political priorities from those in the other countries.

We now turn to families below 25 and those in the ages 45 to 54, that is to the youngest families and to those in what is presumably the economically most active age group. In the latter group, as expected, almost all income is from earnings. Capital income matters very little, and public transfers only make up a few per cent. Young families have roughly the same composition of income as families in the economically most active age group. For families in these age groups, there are only minor differences between countries. But again Sweden (and to some extent the UK) stands out because of the significant role played by public transfers.

Elderly families are distinct, both because the composition of income in the two oldest age groups is very different from that of younger families and because there are striking differences between countries. Overall, the pattern is quite complex:

1. Public transfers and occupational pensions together contribute at least half of pre-tax income. They make up a larger proportion of family income in the European countries than in Canada, Israel and the United States. It is interesting to note that Sweden does not differ from West Germany and Norway in terms of the transfer income share of elderly families.
2. Elderly families generally have some income from economic activity of their own. In some countries, such as Israel, earnings make up a considerable proportion of pre-tax

income. In fact, a fair number of family heads continue to work full time on a full year basis after they have reached 65 years. On the average 7 per cent of heads in the ages 65–74, and 1 per cent of heads in the ages 75 and above, continue to work full time/full year in these seven countries.[2]
3. Capital income is also an important source of income for elderly families. In Canada, Israel and the United States, both capital incomes and earnings are more important than in the other countries.

This examination of income packages in various age groups has indicated important differences between these seven nations. The most significant difference concerns the roles played by factor income (earnings and capital income) and transfer income. Transfer income is most important in Sweden and least important in Canada, Israel and the United States. This difference is largely due to differences among the elderly.

INCOME LEVEL AND DISTRIBUTION

The previous section found that in some countries families are relatively more dependent on markets (earnings and capital) and in others more dependent on politics (transfers). If markets and politics distribute income differently, one would expect to find differences between the countries in the overall distribution of income. This issue is the subject of the next section.

Factor income

Consider first the distribution of income before taxes and transfers. Table 4.2 shows average factor income for families in various age groups, expressed as a proportion of the average for the entire population.[3]

The table shows, as one would expect, that there are substantial differences between age groups in the relative levels of factor income; elderly families in particular have low factor incomes. The differences between age groups are highest in Germany (standard deviation (SD) = 0.63) and lowest in Israel (SD =

Table 4.2 Factor income of different age groups in relation to national mean

	Age							Total	Standard deviation (SD)
	≤24	25-34	35-44	45-54	55-64	65-74	75+		
Canada	0.65	1.07	1.32	1.40	1.06	0.38	0.24	1.00	0.42
West Germany	0.77	1.19	1.59	1.87	1.88	0.12	0.06	1.00	0.63
Israel	0.84	1.18	1.40	1.32	0.99	0.33	0.23	1.00	0.43
Norway	0.70	1.22	1.52	1.50	1.20	0.38	0.07	1.00	0.52
Sweden	0.65	1.25	1.64	1.66	1.21	0.23	0.14	1.00	0.59
United Kingdom	0.86	1.23	1.45	1.58	1.05	0.23	0.14	1.00	0.52
United States	0.61	1.08	1.39	1.45	1.13	0.37	0.23	1.00	0.45
Mean	0.72	1.17	1.47	1.54	1.07	0.29	0.15	—	—
SD	0.09	0.07	0.11	0.17	0.11	0.09	0.07	—	—

1. Factor income = earnings and capital income.
2. The row of SDs measure the cross-national variation, and the column of SDs the variation between the seven age groups.

0.42). On average, factor incomes of the 45–54 groups are more than twice as high as in the under 25 groups and more than ten times as high as in the 75+ groups. These cross-sectional age–income profiles should not be confused with the income trajectories of single individuals. While the data in Table 4.2 display the familiar cross-sectional pattern of a peak income in the mid-40s and declining incomes thereafter, the (longitudinal) income trajectories of single individuals usually do not reach their maximum until just before retirement (cf. Kreps, 1976; Ruggles and Ruggles, 1977).[4]

Net income

Net income is factor income plus public transfers and occupational pensions, and minus direct taxes. The taxes taken into consideration are central and local income taxes and payroll taxes. Employer's social security contributions are not included on the income, transfer or the direct tax side.[5]

The distribution of disposable income over age groups is shown in Table 4.3. Disposable income is below average for the youngest group of families, rises gradually to a peak for families in the ages 35–54. and then falls again to below average for elderly families. Yet, when comparing Tables 4.2 and 4.3 one can see that in all countries disposable family income varies considerably less between age groups than factor income does (the average standard deviation for factor income is 0.51 as compared to an average standard deviation of 0.29 for disposable incomes).

By comparing the distributions in Table 4.2 (pre-tax/transfer income) and Table 4.3 (post-tax/transfer income) one can also get some idea of the redistributive impact of taxes and transfers. As is well known, the difference between such distributions cannot be interpreted as the redistributive effect of the tax/ transfer system since taxes and transfers are likely to affect not only post-tax/transfer incomes, but also incomes before taxes and transfers. Nevertheless, the comparison shows the distributive profile of taxes and transfers in the actual system.

Comparing Tables 4.2 and 4.3 shows, first of all, that families in the youngest age group have more or less the same relative position after, as well as before, taxes and transfers. Second, families aged 25–54 have a lower relative level of post-tax/transfer

Table 4.3 Net income of different age groups in relation to national mean

	≤24	25–34	35–44	45–54	55–64	65–74	75+	Total	Standard deviation (SD)
Canada	0.62	0.99	1.22	1.30	1.06	0.71	0.54	1.00	0.28
West Germany	0.62	0.94	1.25	1.60	0.97	0.63	0.53	1.00	0.36
Israel	0.81	1.09	1.25	1.21	0.97	0.63	0.60	1.00	0.25
Norway	0.68	1.09	1.33	1.27	1.09	0.74	0.51	1.00	0.29
Sweden	0.63	1.13	1.34	1.25	1.08	0.82	0.61	1.00	0.27
United Kingdom	0.86	1.13	1.31	1.37	1.00	0.55	0.44	1.00	0.33
United States	0.60	0.99	1.25	1.33	1.09	0.75	0.57	1.00	0.28
Mean	0.69	1.05	1.28	1.33	1.04	0.69	0.54	—	—
SD	0.10	0.07	0.04	0.12	0.05	0.08	0.05	—	—

Net income = gross income minus direct taxes (including both income taxes and payroll taxes levied on employers).

income than pre-tax/transfer income. Third, families in the two oldest groups have a higher relative income level after than before taxes and transfers. The redistribution between age groups is hence primarily from the middle aged to the elderly. Background data show that in all the countries this redistribution occurs primarily via transfers but also to some degree via taxes, i.e. via lower tax rates relative to pre-tax income for the elderly. (For a detailed analysis on income redistribution between income and demographic groups see Chapter 2.)

Net equivalent income

The previous section described the distribution of income per family. Since families differ in size, however, this is not an adequate measure of standard of living. Two families with the same net income will not have the same standard of living if for instance one is a two-person family and the other is a four-member family. Table 4.1 showed that average family size differs a great deal between countries and between age groups. The use of a measure of net equivalent income in which the income of each family is adjusted for family size (as explained in Chapter 1) provides a more accurate comparison of standards of living.

As seen in Table 4.4, the difference between age groups are most pronounced in West Germany and the United Kingdom, and least pronounced in Israel and Canada. However, differences between age groups are much smaller with the equivalent income measure than without this adjustment; the adjusted standard deviations are only about half the size of the unadjusted ones. The table particularly illustrates that if family size is not adjusted for, the relative economic position of the elderly is clearly underestimated. Elderly families are smaller than average, so that their relative standard of living is much higher than indicated by their unadjusted net income. On the basis of the unadjusted net income (Table 4.3), the economic welfare level of the two oldest groups was estimated to be no more than 69 and 54 per cent of the population average. After adjusting for family size the relative economic levels of these groups are up to 92 and 80 per cent of the average.

There are noticeable differences between the countries in the relative economic status of families in the various age groups.

Table 4.4 Equivalent net income of different age groups in relation to national mean

	≤24	25–34	35–44	45–54	55–64	65–74	75+	Total	Standard deviation (SD)
Canada	0.87	0.96	0.96	1.11	1.15	0.94	0.81	1.00	0.11
West Germany	0.86	0.88	0.94	1.30	1.07	0.84	0.77	1.00	0.17
Israel	1.02	1.03	0.91	1.00	1.23	0.92	0.96	1.00	0.10
Norway	0.81	0.96	0.99	1.04	1.18	1.01	0.79	1.00	0.12
Sweden	0.86	1.00	0.98	1.12	1.17	0.96	0.78	1.00	0.13
United Kingdom	0.99	0.97	0.97	1.20	1.17	0.76	0.67	1.00	0.18
United States	0.77	0.93	0.95	1.13	1.21	0.99	0.84	1.00	0.14
Mean	0.88	0.96	0.96	1.13	1.17	0.92	0.80	—	—
SD	0.08	0.04	0.02	0.09	0.05	0.08	0.08	—	—

The adjustment of net income for family size is done with the use of the following equivalence scale:

Number of family members:	1	2	3	4	...	10+
Equivalence factor:	0.50	0.75	1.00	1.25	...	3.00

Among elderly families, the most striking feature is how far behind their compatriots in the other countries are the elderly in the UK. The relative adjusted disposabie income of the 65–74 group in the UK around 1980 was only 76 per cent of the population average, and in the 75+ group it was as low as 67 per cent. These figures should be compared to 94 per cent and 82 per cent which are the averages of the elderly's relative incomes in the other six nations. The highest relative standard of living of elderly families is in Israel.

All of the analyses have shown traces of a Rowntree type of cycle in the distribution of income over age groups. This pattern is very clear in terms of factor income, but much less pronounced for net income. Although one cannot make any direct inference about redistributive impact on the basis of these kinds of analysis, the results strongly suggest that transfers and taxes have a redistributive profile which favours marginal labour market groups, most notably the elderly.

When net income is adjusted for differences in family size, the cycle is further modified. It can still be seen but there are a number of exceptions to the expected pattern, and in one case – Israel – there is no cyclical pattern at all. In terms of economic well-being, therefore, it appears that the Rowntree type of cycle still tends to occur, but that its presence is neither strong nor universal.

Inequality

Having looked only at differences *between* age groups, the analysis now turns to inequalities *within* these groups. The degree of inequality in the distribution of incomes can be expressed by a range of measures, each differing in its sensitivity to income variations at different levels of the income distribution.[6] The most popular inequality measures, as well as the one used in this chapter, is the Gini coefficient, which ranges in value between 0 and 1; the higher the coefficient, the greater the degree of measured inequality.

Table 4.5 gives Gini coefficients for the distribution of net equivalent income within separate age groups as well as for the entire population. As Chapter 2 indicated, overall income is most

Table 4.5 Gini coefficients for the distribution of equivalent net income

	≤24	25–34	35–44	45–54	55–64	65–74	75+	Total	Standard deviation (SD)
Canada	0.332	0.295	0.285	0.286	0.296	0.309	0.291	0.299	0.016
West Germany	0.304	0.267	0.317	0.452	0.342	0.298	0.340	0.355	0.055
Israel	0.304	0.278	0.330	0.344	0.342	0.360	0.429	0.333	0.044
Norway	0.296	0.249	0.214	0.229	0.229	0.250	0.229	0.243	0.025
Sweden	0.236	0.209	0.192	0.216	0.195	0.143	0.126	0.205	0.037
United Kingdom	0.279	0.264	0.253	0.246	0.253	0.266	0.240	0.273	0.012
United States	0.345	0.313	0.304	0.303	0.331	0.342	0.355	0.326	0.019
Mean	0.300	0.268	0.271	0.297	0.284	0.281	0.287	0.291	—
SD	0.033	0.031	0.049	0.076	0.055	0.067	0.092	0.050	—

unequally distributed in West Germany, Israel and the United States and most equally distributed in Sweden, followed by Norway, the United Kingdom and Canada.

The cross-national variation in the degree of income inequality – as measured by standard deviations – is considerably higher among the elderly than among younger cohorts (the only exception is for the age groups 45–54 years where an extraordinarily high level of inequality in West Germany causes the difference between countries in this age group to be 'abnormally' high). While the highest Gini coefficient for the total populations is 1.7 times as high as the lowest one, in the 65–74 age group the gap is 2.5, and in the 75+ group it is 3.4. Hence, in explaining cross-national differences in income inequality, extra attention needs to be paid to the process of income attainment in old age and its cross-national variability.

Poverty

Although the concept of poverty is controversial, most social scientists agree that the group with the lowest income can be defined as poor even in affluent societies. In this chapter, the poor are defined as all persons belonging to families with a net equivalent income below half the median for all families. Although somewhat arbitrarily chosen, this poverty definition has become common in recent years. Table 4.6 shows the extent of poverty in different age groups according to this definition.

On average, in these seven countries, about one out of every ten persons belongs to a family with an income below the poverty line. The overall figure is highest in the United States (about 17 per cent) followed by Israel and Canada, and lowest in Norway and Sweden (about 5 per cent).[7] The poverty rates in different age groups follow a Rowntree type of cycle: the risk of poverty is highest in the youngest and oldest groups. But this cycle does not appear in all countries. In Canada and Israel, the risk of poverty is comparatively high in all groups, but no Rowntree type of cycle exists. In Sweden, the risk of poverty is generally low and is virtually non-existent in the oldest groups.

Because of the way poverty is defined here, the poverty rate within a specific age group is a function of both its relative income level and the way these incomes are distributed within the group.

Table 4.6 Poverty rates

	≤24	25–34	35–44	45–54	55–64	65–74	75+	Total	Standard deviation (SD)
Canada	22.7	13.1	11.8	9.5	10.6	11.2	12.1	12.1	4.1
West Germany	14.5	7.2	4.2	4.5	7.3	12.7	15.2	7.2	4.3
Israel	11.7	8.9	17.4	14.5	11.0	22.6	27.1	14.5	6.1
Norway	16.8	5.5	3.5	3.5	3.3	2.7	7.3	4.8	4.6
Sweden	17.3	4.8	5.3	5.6	3.9	0.0	0.0	5.0	5.4
United Kingdom	11.6	7.9	7.3	5.2	5.6	16.2	22.0	8.8	5.8
United States	28.0	17.4	16.0	13.2	13.7	17.8	25.5	16.9	5.3
Mean	17.5	9.3	9.4	8.0	7.9	11.9	15.6	9.9	—
SD	5.5	4.2	5.3	4.1	3.7	7.5	9.2	4.4	—

The poverty rate is defined as the proportion (per cent) of persons belonging to families with an equivalent net income below half of the median for all families.

To illustrate, compare the USA and the UK, where elderly poverty rates are about the same. However, Table 4.4 indicated that the elderly in the United States have a considerably higher relative income level than do the elderly in the UK, while Table 4.5 showed that incomes are more unequally distributed among the elderly in the USA than in the UK. It seems, therefore, that in the United States the high poverty rate among the elderly is due mainly to the unequal distribution of income among them, whereas in the UK the same poverty rate results mainly from the low income level of the elderly relative to other age groups.

In general, the poverty rate of a specific age group will differ from the national poverty rate if the average income level (mean equivalent net income) of the group is different from the national average, or if the distribution of income at the bottom tail is different (or both, unless the two differences should happen to cancel each other out). By comparing Tables 4.4 and 4.6, it can be seen that the poverty rate of a specific group is generally higher than the national poverty rate when its average income level is lower. But there are a number of cases which do not fit this pattern. This means that there must be differences in the distribution of income within age groups that result in a difference between observed and 'expected' poverty rates.[8] For example consider the following:

1. In Canada, the poverty rates in the two oldest age groups are not higher than the national average although the income level is lower. This means that income distribution is less inegalitarian at the bottom tail among the elderly than in the general population.
2. In Sweden, poverty as defined here has been eliminated among the elderly but not in the entire population, which is to say that, as in Canada, there is less inequality among the elderly than in the general population.
3. In the UK, the poverty rate in the youngest age group is higher than the national poverty rate although the relative income levels are the same. Consequently, there must be more inequality among the young.
4. In Israel, the elderly have the highest relative income level

but also the highest rate of poverty of all these countries. This implies that there must be exceptional inequality in the distribution of income among the elderly in Israel.

INCOME PACKAGING AND DISTRIBUTION

So far it has been observed that the relative economic position of different age groups as well as the overall distribution of income varies a great deal from one country to another, and that public transfers make up different proportions of family income in these seven countries. The analysis now turns to possible relationships between these two phenomena, i.e. to the relationship between income packaging and income distribution. It is hypothesised that, in a comparison between industrial nations, the higher the relative level of public transfers, the less inequality in the distribution of income.

The analysis seeks neither to explain differences in inequality nor to determine how public transfers affect the final distribution of income. To do either presents formidable methodological and theoretical problems which go beyond the scope of this study, whose goals are much more modest. It examines to what extent the cross-national pattern corresponds to one that would be found if high transfer levels reduced income inequality. If such a pattern is found, this will be taken as a sign that such a causal relationship *might* be in operation.

Figure 4.2 shows the correlations across these seven nations of the relative level of public transfers and measures of inequality. Three measures of inequality are used, the Gini coefficient, the poverty rate and the relative income of elderly families. In each case the data are equivalent net income. The diagram gives a mixed picture.

The first two scattergrams suggest that the cross-national variation in income inequality and poverty rates can be partly explained by differences in the proportion of public transfers in the family income package. The more important public transfers are, on average, the more equally distributed incomes are ($r = -0.70$), and the lower poverty rates are ($r = -0.77$). The

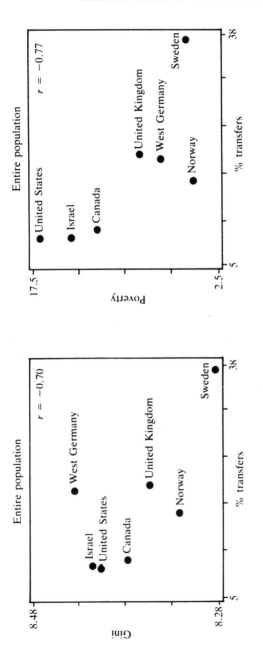

Figure 4.2 Public transfers and inequality. (Percentage transfers are public transfers as a percentage of total income. All inequality measures are based on the equivalent net income.)

continued

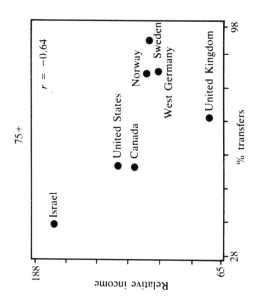

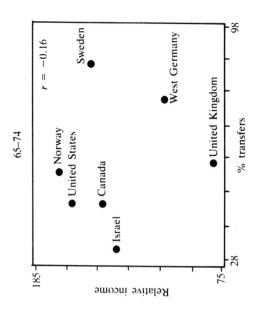

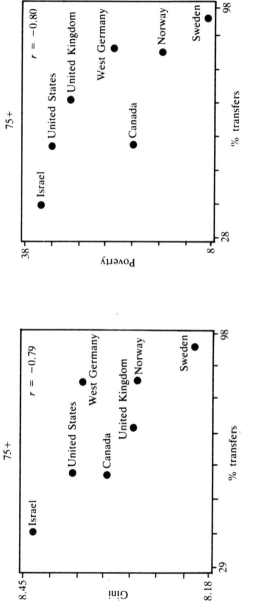

Figure 4.2 continued

exceptions to this general rule are West Germany, where incomes are quite unequally distributed even though transfers represent a significant proportion of family income, and Norway, where the poverty rate is lower than one would expect on the basis of the transfer rate. However, the visual pattern suggests that the high correlation to a large extent is influenced by a single outlier: Sweden. If Sweden were excluded from the comparisons, the correlations would drop considerably. These results hence give some support for our hypothesis, but far from any clear confirmation.

About half of all public transfers in these countries go to elderly families, though only about 15 per cent of the population reside in these families.[9] Therefore, one would expect that cross-national differences in the economic status of elderly families would be closely related to the relative role of public transfers. Further, to the extent that the hypothesis about the redistributive impact of public transfers is true, one would expect elderly families to be better off in countries where public transfers play a greater role. However, the correlation between the level of public transfers and the relative income of the elderly is either virtually non-existent or it suggests that the elderly tend to be better off in countries with *lower* transfer levels (see the middle two scattergrams in Figure 4.2). The hypothesis is consequently not supported by the data.

The two final scattergrams in Figure 4.2, however, do support the hypothesis that poverty rates and measured income equality within elderly families are generally lower in countries where public transfer accounts for a larger proportion of the elderly's pre-tax income. (This is also true for the 65–74 group which is not included in the diagram.)

Overall income inequality may tend to be lower in countries with higher transfer levels, but this is not demonstrated more than suggestively in the data and does not apply to inequality between elderly and non-elderly families. On the other hand, inequality within elderly families is clearly lower in countries where the elderly have a comparatively larger part of their income from public transfers. Thus, the data have demonstrated that the relationship between public transfers and inequality is rather more complex than anticipated.

CONCLUSIONS

This study is based on seven microdata sets which have been carefully rearranged to secure the highest possible cross-national comparability. A project like the Luxemburg Income Study begs the question: Does the improvement in data quality make a difference compared with the use of pre-published statistics?

It is usually not easy to answer this kind of question since one can seldom directly compare results from two different studies. However, in this case there is the rare possibility of making such a comparison. Radner (1985) compared the distribution of income over age groups in Canada, Israel, Norway and the United States. He used data from the same sources as are in the LIS database, and the same key definitions of income and family units are used. The main differences between the two studies is that Radner has based his study on tables published in each country, while this chapter has used the LIS microdata files. Table 4.7 compares Radner's data and LIS data on the relative economic status (total pre-tax family income) of different age groups.[10]

Since the Canadian, Israeli and US data in the two studies refer to different years, the direct comparison is limited to the Norwegian data. The LIS data show a considerably lower income level for the youngest Norwegian age group, and a much higher relative income for middle aged families than do the Radner data. The cross-sectional age–income profile for Norway appears to be much flatter in Radner's study than in the LIS data. Radner's results suggest that Norway is the country with least inequality between age groups, while the LIS data suggest that both Canada and Israel have flatter age–income profiles than does Norway. Using pre-published statistics as Radner did, rather than rearranged microdata files as in the LIS project, leads to different substantive conclusions. It is clear, therefore, that method does matter.

The main findings and conclusions have been pointed out during the chapter and need not be repeated here. It is, however, worth noting the importance of the economic status of elderly families in explaining the differences and inequalities that have been identified. The differences between countries in income packaging are to a large degree functions of differences in the

Table 4.7 Total gross income of different age groups in relation to national mean

	≤24	25–34	35–44	45–54	55–64	65+	Total	Standard deviation (SD)
LIS results:								
Canada (1981)	0.61	1.00	1.25	1.32	1.05	0.60	1.00	0.28
Israel (1979)	0.81	1.11	1.32	1.25	0.98	0.51	1.00	0.27
Norway (1979)	0.65	1.09	1.36	1.34	1.14	0.56	1.00	0.31
United States (1979)	0.58	0.99	1.28	1.36	1.13	0.60	1.00	0.31
Mean	0.66	1.05	1.30	1.32	1.08	0.57	—	—
SD	0.09	0.05	0.04	0.04	0.06	0.04	—	—
Radner's results:								
Canada (1979)	0.63	1.07	1.29	1.34	1.09	0.57	1.00	0.30
Israel (1981)	0.69	1.14	1.30	1.33	1.05	0.48	1.00	0.31
Norway (1979)	0.75	0.99	1.24	1.31	1.17	0.53	1.00	0.28
United States (1980)	0.57	0.97	1.28	1.39	1.17	0.63	1.00	0.31
Mean	0.66	1.04	1.28	1.34	1.12	0.55	—	—
SD	0.07	0.07	0.02	0.03	0.05	0.05	—	—

Sources: LIS data and Radner (1985).

relative importance of factor and transfer incomes for the elderly. There are generally more differences between countries in measures such as relative standards of living, degrees of income inequality, and levels of poverty when the comparison is confined to elderly families than when the total population is compared. Similarly, inequalities within countries are to a considerable degree a result of differentials between elderly and non-elderly families. This suggests that the process of income generation for elderly families is of particular importance for the understanding both of inequalities within and of differences between countries in the distribution of income.

NOTES

This chapter is part of a research programme that has been supported by grants from the Swedish Delegation for Social Research, the Norwegian Ministry of Consumer Affairs and Government Administration (Department of Income Policy), the Government of Luxemburg, the National Institute of Aging (Washington, DC) and the Ford Foundation. Preliminary versions of the chapter were presented at the Brookdale Institute of Gerontology and Human Development, Jerusalem, and the first Luxemburg Income Study Conference. We wish to thank Greg Duncan, Barbara Hobson, Huib van de Stadt and our colleagues at the Institute for Social Research, Stockholm, and within the Luxemburg Income Study for their useful comments.

1. As it is not the intention to explain fully the distribution of income within each of these countries, the chapter has brought into the analysis information on the history and traditions of each society or on their economic, social and political institutions.
2. Earnings also comprise a large proportion of family income among Norwegian families in the 65–74 age group. This is explained by the relatively high retirement age in that country, normally between 67 and 70 years.
3. Factor income roughly corresponds to income from market activity. However, it would have been preferable to include occupational pensions in this table so that it would show the distribution of market income more accurately. But, since occupational pensions cannot be separated from social pensions in the Swedish data, this is not possible on a comparative basis.
4. The results in Table 4.2 suggest that West Germany is a case of its own, with exceptionally high levels of factor income for families in the age groups 45–64 and exceptionally low levels for the two oldest groups. This indicates a more 'complete' retirement in West Germany

and a different distribution of market income over the life cycle than in the other countries. It is likely that West Germany would look more like the other countries if lifetime income, rather than annual income, were compared.

5. This is a weakness in the data. In most countries, social security contributions are derived in part from a payroll tax paid by employees and in part from an employer's contribution. But how the contributions are divided between these components differs from country to country, and in the case of Sweden the total social security contribution is carried by the employer. From the point of view of this analysis these differences are arbitrary and it would have improved the comparability of the material if employers' contributions had been included. As a point of illustration, the inclusion of employers' social security contributions as an element of both gross income and direct taxes raises the average level of income taxation relative to total pre-tax income in Norway and Sweden from 24 to 32 per cent and 30 to 44 per cent, respectively (cf. Ringen, 1986).

6. See Cowell (1977), Allison (1978) and Schwartz and Winship (1980) for overviews of the most commonly used inequality measures and their properties.

7. The poverty rate among the young families in Sweden is probably exaggerated because of the Swedish family definition (see Table 4.1, note 1). This also exaggerates somewhat the overall level of poverty in Sweden. For a fuller analysis of poverty using the LIS data, see Chapter 3.

8. This difference in income distribution is not necessarily reflected in the Gini coefficients since the Gini is a measure of overall inequality which is not particularly sensitive to income differences at the bottom tail of the distribution.

9. Population shares and public transfer shares of families aged 65+:

	Canada	West Germany	Israel	Norway	Sweden	United Kingdom	United States
Percentage of population:	11	19	13	16	18	16	13
Percentage of transfers:	46	60	35	59	49	38	58
Difference:	4.2	3.2	2.7	3.7	2.7	2.4	4.5

10. Total pre-tax family income is the only direct comparison that can be made between the two studies.

5 · RETIREMENT AND WELL-BEING AMONG THE ELDERLY

Lea Achdut and Yossi Tamir

INTRODUCTION

During the past two decades a massive growth has taken place in social security expenditure in industrialised countries. From 1960 to the beginning of the 1980s expenditure on social security increased almost twice as much as gross national product. The rise was particularly marked in transfer payments to the elderly, which became the main component in total social security expenditure in most developed nations. The real increase in expenditure on old-age pensions in OECD countries continued also after the economic crisis which hit the western nations in the mid 1970s. In the early 1980s public expenditure on old age pensions, for example, amounted to around 12 per cent of GDP in West Germany and Sweden, over 7 per cent in the United Kingdom and over 5 per cent in the USA (OECD, 1985). Against the background of these spending trends, it is particularly interesting to study the economic well-being of the elderly at the beginning of the 1980s in a comparative perspective.

The well-being of the elderly population and its various sub-groups in each of the countries depends on many factors, such as the usual retirement age, the degree of flexibility and liberality with regard to the pension age, the generosity of the social security retirement programmes, the role of occupational pension arrangements in the general system of income maintenance for the elderly, and the patterns of living arrangements for old persons (e.g. living alone, living with their children). The purpose of this chapter, however, is not to present a detailed description of these institutional characteristics but rather to provide a comparative empirical analysis of the economic well-being of the elderly population in the LIS countries.

The vast literature on theoretical and empirical measures of inequality and poverty – e.g. Atkinson (1983), Danziger and Taussig (1977, 1979) and Danziger et al. (1982) – has examined the issues involved in defining the alternative measures of well-being in depth. It concentrates on the different treatments of the 'income' concepts (for example, consumption versus income measures, and income before direct taxes versus net income) and of the recipient unit concepts (household versus adjustment for unit size).

Since measures of non-cash income, wealth, consumption, savings and other indicators of well-being have not yet been incorporated in the LIS project, this chapter focuses on cash income components. It analyses family cash incomes and uses equivalent income to measure inequality and poverty.

An important question arising in a comparative study of the aged is how to define a 'retired family'. Because of intercountry variations in pensionable age and in the work patterns of the elderly, the usual demographic definition of retirement (65+ years) contains some arbitrariness and is problematic within the context of a family income study. Therefore, this chapter uses alternative definitions of retirement, based not only on the age of the family head, but also on the composition of family income. The common denominator of these definitions is the age of 55 years and over for the family head, whilst the differences among them stem from the different possible combinations of family income, in particular different ratios of earnings to retirement income.

The first part of the chapter describes the demographic characteristics of the elderly population, and the following part discusses the problem of defining a 'retired family' and compares the size of the retired population according to alternative definitions. The third part analyses the relative contribution of each of the income sources to the standard of living of elderly families in general and of retired families according to one of the alternative definitions, while the fourth part examines the inequality of the distribution of income both between and within the various age groups. The fifth section deals with the incidence of poverty and the composition of the poor population.

The chapter concludes with a discussion of the interrelationships among several issues examined earlier. It focuses on the size of the retired population and its income composition as affected by institutional and demographic characteristics and on the possible connection between income composition and the nature of income distribution.

DEMOGRAPHIC CHARACTERISTICS OF ELDERLY FAMILIES

This chapter uses a detailed breakdown of elderly families into four groups according to the head's age: 55–59, 60–64, 65–74 and 75 and over. Table 5.1 shows that the distribution of families by the age of family head varies considerably among the countries surveyed.[1] The percentage of all families whose head is aged 55+ is significantly higher in Norway, West Germany and the United Kingdom. In Canada and the United States, the corresponding percentage is the lowest, whilst Sweden and Israel are in the middle of the scale even though they are nearer to the former group.

If the more usual definition, i.e. families whose head is 65 and over, is used, the ranking of the countries remains essentially unchanged. The variance among the countries is most outstanding

Table 5.1 Percentage distribution of families by age of head

Country	\u2264 54	55+	55–59	60–64	65–74	75+	Total population
			Age of head				
Norway	55.5	44.5	9.0	8.3	15.2	12.1	100.0
West Germany	56.6	43.4	8.3	5.9	17.5	11.7	100.0
United Kingdom	57.8	42.2	9.2	6.9	16.8	9.2	100.0
Sweden	59.7	40.3	6.6	7.9	14.1	11.6	100.0
Israel	60.8	39.2	8.2	8.2	15.6	7.2	100.0
United States	65.7	34.3	7.9	6.9	12.0	7.5	100.0
Canada	68.5	31.5	7.6	6.7	10.6	6.6	100.0

Table 5.2 Family type by age of family head

Family type	Norway 55+	Norway 65–74	Norway 75+	West Germany 55+	West Germany 65–74	West Germany 75+	United Kingdom 55+	United Kingdom 65–74	United Kingdom 75+	Sweden 55+	Sweden 65–74	Sweden 75+	Israel 55+	Israel 65–74	Israel 75+	United States 55+	United States 65–74	United States 75+	Canada 55+	Canada 65–74	Canada 75+
Total	100	100	100	100	100	100	100	100	100	100	100	100	100	100	100	100	100	100	100	100	100
Single male	14	14	18	7	7	11	11	11	13	17	18	17	6	7	11	9	9	12	11	11	14
Single female	33	35	52	41	44	51	29	31	47	38	37	57	21	26	23	28	31	44	26	29	45
Couple without children	34	41	25	35	36	33	38	43	25	42	44	26	41	46	47	38	42	30	34	40	28
Families with children[1]	19	11	5	5	1	—	5	1	—	3	1	—	12	7	5	8	5	2	9	4	1
Other[2]	—	—	—	12	11	5	17	13	15	—	—	—	20	14	14	17	13	12	20	16	12
Average family size	2.3	2.0	1.5	2.1	1.9	1.6	2.4	2.1	1.9	1.7	1.7	1.4	3.2	3.0	2.2	2.6	2.3	1.9	2.7	2.3	1.9

1. This type of family includes couples, one-parent families and families with children and additional adult persons. Children are persons under 18 years of age.
2. All families without children which are not included in the first three types.

in the oldest age group, 75 and over. In Norway, the percentage of families in this age group is almost double that in Canada.

Table 5.2 shows the family composition of the elderly and, as might be expected, indicates that couples without children and single females are the two main groups among elderly families. In the 55–59, 60–64 and 65–74 age groups, couples without children constitute the largest group even though the proportion of single females increases significantly with age, mainly at the expense of the families with children group. In the 75+ age group the situation is reversed. In all the countries, except Israel, the percentage of single females is higher than that of couples without children. In Sweden, Norway and West Germany, single females are slightly over 50 per cent of all families in the 75+ age group; in the United States, Canada and the United Kingdom, 45–46 per cent. In Israel only 23 per cent of all families in the 75+ age group are single females, whereas the percentage of couples without children is double at 47 per cent. This difference between Israel and the other countries apparently stems from the former's relatively low rates of divorce and separation. The lowest percentage of single males in the 75+ age group is to be found in Israel and West Germany (approximately 11 per cent) and the highest in Sweden and Norway (17–18 per cent).

Another difference among the countries relates to the family type termed 'other'. This consists of households of old persons without children who live with other adults who are related to the family head or spouse. In Israel and Canada approximately 20 per cent of elderly families in the 55+ age group belong to this category, in the United States and the United Kingdom about 17 per cent, and in Germany around 11 per cent. This family type is more prevalent in the younger groups (55–64) than in the older (65+) ones.[2] Thus, as late as 1981 a significant group of older persons lived in an extended family. For instance, because of shared living arrangements Israeli elderly families are larger than in other countries (3.2 persons on the average, per family). Conversely, Sweden is characterised by the smallest average family size – 1.7. The order of the countries by family size is the same in all age groups. Hence the rankings of countries by the share of elderly are robust whether 'old' means age 55, 65, 75 or older.

WHO ARE THE RETIRED ELDERLY?

The various definitions of a 'retired family' used in this chapter are based on two elements: the age of the family head and the income composition of the family. From an economic point of view, there are two basic criteria for defining retirement – the extent of participation in the labour market and the existence of pension income (which may come from social security or from an occupational pension scheme). One can define a retired family on the basis of either one of these criteria or by combinations of them.

Five alternative definitions of a retired family are given here. All refer to families whose head is 55 years old and over, but they differ from each other with regard to the family's income sources and composition:

1. Complete retirement from the labour market, i.e. family with zero earnings.
2. A family with pension income.
3. A family with zero earnings but with pension income.
4. A family whose pension income exceeds its earnings (subsumes definition 3).
5. A family with pension income whose earnings do not exceed a quarter of its net income.

Definition 3 is the narrowest definition, whereas 2 is the broadest. However, a definition which includes both earnings and retirement income (such as 4 or 5) is more suitable for the purposes of this analysis since some older people continue working even after they are entitled to retirement income. Further, since the family is the income unit, even if one family member has completely retired from the labour market, others may still have some earnings.

Definition 5 is chosen as the primary definition since in limiting earnings in relation to total income, rather than simply in relation to pensions, it takes into account the role of other income sources, such as property income, which are likely to be important for at least some retired people. Hereafter, a family meeting this primary definition will be referred to as 'retired'.

The definition of retired is important because of the trend towards early retirement in the major western countries. Early retirement coupled with longer life expectancy at older ages can create large increases in retirement expenditures. If age of retirement is an important policy issue, therefore, the definition of retirement must first be specified. Our intent is to add precision to an area where it is sorely needed.

Table 5.3 shows the proportion of retired families in the various age groups according to each of these five definitions. The findings referring to the group below the "normal" retirement age of 65 are of special interest. They reveal that Sweden has, on the one hand, the highest percentage of families (55 per cent) with pension income in the 55–64 age group, but, on the other hand, the lowest percentage of families (15 per cent) without any earnings at all. Hence Swedish retirement may be more gradual than retirement in other countries. Israel resembles Sweden in having a high percentage of families (35 per cent) with pension income along with a low percentage of families (16 per cent) with zero earnings. West Germany is also characterised by a relatively high percentage of families (44 per cent) with pension income, but unlike Sweden and other LIS countries, it has a high percentage of families with zero earnings (35 per cent). Comparing the proportions of families with pension income and those with pension income *and* zero earnings reveals that Sweden and Israel have relatively more working families with pension income, whereas in West Germany most of the families receiving pension income do not work at all. Hence retirement is more abrupt in West Germany than in other nations.

The United States, Canada and the United Kingdom have more or less the same percentage of families in the 55–64 age group with zero earnings, but they differ in the percentage with pension income. The USA has the lowest percentage among LIS countries of these families with pension income (17 per cent), whereas Canada and the United Kingdom are in the middle of the range. The US figure probably reflects the fact that they have no 'early retirement' system. According to the other definitions, which combine earnings with pension income, West Germany has the highest percentage of retired families followed by Sweden, whilst the United States and Canada have relatively fewest. Thus we might expect that West Germany would be most pressed by pensions as a percentage of social expenditures. OECD (1985) estimates indicate that this is indeed the case.

Table 5.3 The proportion of retired families within age group according to the various definitions

Percentage of families	Norway¹ 55–64	Norway¹ 65–74	Norway¹ 75+	West Germany 55–64	West Germany 65–74	West Germany 75+	United Kingdom 55–64	United Kingdom 65–74	United Kingdom 75+	Sweden 55–64	Sweden 65–74	Sweden 75+	Israel 55–64	Israel 65–74	Israel 75+	United States 55–64	United States 65–74	United States 75+	Canada 55–64	Canada 65–74	Canada 75+
1. Primary definition	—	—	—	27	79	89	15	77	90	21	83	98	16	63	86	8	66	84	10	73	90
2. With zero earnings	14	47	86	35	83	95	19	72	89	14	66	90	16	58	80	18	61	83	17	64	85
3. With some retirement income	—	—	—	44	91	92	26	98	99	55	100	100	35	94	100	17	91	95	25	98	99
4. With both no earnings and some retirement income	—	—	—	26	75	87	14	71	88	14	66	90	14	58	80	6	57	79	8	64	85
5. With retirement income greater than earnings	—	—	—	31	82	89	19	84	91	29	94	99	17	68	88	8	74	87	11	78	91

1. The data on the retirement income in Norway contain only private pensions: therefore this variable is not reliable, and we cannot compare Norway with the other countries.

In all of these countries almost everyone in the two older age groups has pension income, and the differences among the countries are due to different proportions of families with earnings. Israel, the USA and Canada have relatively high proportions of elderly families with earnings, particularly compared to West Germany and the United Kingdom. In Israel 42 per cent of the families in the 65–74 age group and 20 per cent of those in the 75+ age group have some earnings, most of which exceed a quarter of their net income. The corresponding percentages in West Germany are 17 per cent and 5 per cent. Sweden also has a relatively high percentage of families with earnings but, in contrast to Israel and the United States, the earnings of these families do not generally exceed a quarter of their net income.

THE RELATIVE IMPORTANCE OF THE VARIOUS INCOME SOURCES

One of the important dimensions according to which the economic status of the elderly in various countries can be compared is the composition of gross income. This section examines the contribution of the various income sources, focusing particularly on the roles of transfer income and market income (which includes earnings, property income and occupational pension income).

All elderly families

Table 5.4 presents the distribution of gross income by its components for all the elderly population and for the elderly in the 65–74 and 75+ age groups. In all countries, except Sweden, market income is the main component of the income of families in the 55+ age group, particularly in countries with relatively young populations: Israel, the United States and Canada. Market income constitutes 85 per cent of gross income in Israel and 79 per cent in Canada and the United States. On the other hand, in Sweden and West Germany, whose populations are relatively old, the relative share of market income is low: 46 per cent and 53 per cent respectively. In Norway and the United Kingdom, market income contributes 69 per cent of total income.

Table 5.4 Composition of gross income by income types (all elderly units)

Income type	Norway[1]			West Germany			United Kingdom			Sweden			Israel			United States			Canada		
	55+	65–74	75+	55+	65–74	75+	55+	65–74	75+	55+	65–74	75+	55+	65–74	75+	55+	65–74	75+	55+	65–74	75+
Market income	69	54	24	53	31	24	69	51	39	46	21	15	85	75	68	79	63	53	79	62	51
Earnings	61	41	6	43	17	8	54	26	17	39	12	2	64	42	21	58	32	17	56	28	13
Property income	5	6	8	2	2	4	7	10	10	7	9	13	10	13	22	13	18	24	17	22	30
Occupational pension	3	7	10	8	12	12	8	15	12	—	—	—	11	20	25	8	13	12	6	12	8
Transfer income	31	46	76	47	68	76	31	49	61	54	79	85	15	25	32	21	37	47	20	37	47
Direct taxes	23	19	8	13	5	4	15	11	8	30	28	17	22	14	9	18	11	8	12	9	7
Net income	77	81	92	87	95	96	85	89	92	70	72	83	78	86	91	82	89	92	88	91	93

An examination of the types of income that constitute market income reveals that the relative share of earnings and of occupational pensions is highest in Israel. In the United States and Canada, income from property (13 and 17 per cent of gross income respectively) is particularly prominent whilst the relative importance of earnings is not very different from that in the United Kingdom and Norway. The measured share of market income in Sweden is low not only because of the low share of earnings, but also because of the absence in the Swedish dataset of any separate data on income from occupational pensions.

The average rate of taxation imposed on the elderly is highest in Sweden (30 per cent) and lowest in Canada and West Germany (12 and 13 per cent respectively).[3] In Israel and Norway elderly persons also pay relatively high taxes, approximately 23 per cent of gross income.

The data on the income composition of families in the 65–74 and 75+ age groups show the fall in the relative contribution of market income as the family head's age rises, particularly in Sweden, Norway and West Germany. Market income constitutes only 15 per cent of the gross income of families in the 75+ age group in Sweden, and is less than a quarter in West Germany and Norway. In contrast, the findings for Israel, the United States and Canada appear somewhat surprising since market income in these countries is still the main component in the income of families in the highest age group. In Israel market income accounts for about two-thirds of gross income, while in the United States and Canada gross income is almost equally divided between market and transfer components.

An examination of the various components of market income reveals that about one-third of the gross income of families in the 75+ age group in Canada and nearly a quarter of the income of these families in the United States and Israel come from property, and that the share of property income is greater for this age group than for younger groups. This relative importance of income from property may have a number of explanations: first of all, studies on old persons' saving behaviour have indicated that old persons continue to save after retirement, so that their accumulated property grows as they get older. Secondly, there may have been a greater tendency for older cohorts to accumulate assets since pension systems, especially the occupational ones,

Table 5.5 Composition of gross income by income types (only 'retired' units)

Income type	Norway[1] 55+	65–74	75+	West Germany 55+	65–74	75+	United Kingdom 55+	65–74	75+	Sweden 55+	65–74	75+	Israel 55+	65–74	75+	United States 55+	65–74	75+	Canada 55+	65–74	75+
Market income	38	39	37	16	17	16	32	34	28	11	11	13	58	58	62	49	47	43	49	47	45
Earnings	2	3	1	1	1	–	1	1	–	1	2	1	2	1	1	1	2	1	1	1	1
Property income	9	8	9	2	2	3	11	11	13	10	9	12	25	26	30	26	25	28	31	29	34
Occupational pension	27	28	27	13	14	13	20	22	5	–	–	–	31	31	31	22	20	14	16	16	10
Transfer income	62	61	63	84	83	84	68	66	72	89	89	87	42	42	38	50	52	56	49	51	53
Direct taxes	11	12	10	1	1	1	7	7	6	21	25	17	2	2	2	6	5	4	6	6	6
Net income	89	88	90	99	99	99	93	93	94	79	75	83	98	98	98	94	95	96	94	94	95

were less developed. Thirdly, it may be that in absolute terms income from property does not rise, but that its relative share of gross income increases due to reduction in the contributions of other income sources.

Retired families

Table 5.5 presents the income composition of 'retired' families according to the primary definition of retired used here – a family for whom earnings account for less than a quarter of net income. The data reveal only small differences among the various age groups within each country, suggesting that this population is quite homogeneous within countries. As can be seen, in all countries 'retired' families have almost no earnings (0–2 per cent of gross income) regardless of age group. While this definition of retired restricts the earnings share, it would still allow it to be significantly higher. This suggests that below some threshold level paid work ceases completely, rather than slowly tailing away to nothing. By contrast, the greater relative importance of property income for the 'retired' as compared to the 'elderly' is clear in Canada, the United States and Israel (especially among younger families), whilst the greater relative share of occupational pensions is marked in all the countries.

In Sweden and West Germany transfer income constitutes the largest part of 'retired' families' gross incomes: 89 and 84 per cent respectively, while in Norway and the UK it provides about two-thirds. It contributes around a half of gross incomes in the two North American countries and is least important in Israel at 42 per cent of gross income. In all countries, except Sweden, 'retired' families pay a very low average rate of tax, ranging from 1 per cent in West Germany to 11 per cent in Norway. This contrasts with the 21 per cent rate in Sweden.

DISTRIBUTIONAL CHARACTERISTICS OF ELDERLY FAMILIES' INCOMES

The characteristics of the income distribution of elderly families within and across countries will be analysed from two viewpoints. The first examines the relative economic status within the elderly

Table 5.6 Relative mean net income and relative mean equivalent[1] net income by age of head (all elderly families and only retired families[2])

Age of head	Norway		West Germany		United Kingdom		Sweden		Israel		United States		Canada	
	all[4]	ret.[5]	all	ret.	all	ret.	all	ret.	all	ret.	all	ret.	all	ret.
Mean net income:														
Total 55+	100	91	100	79	100	58	100	81	100	64	100	68	100	63
55–59	144	—	156	81	158	60	136	85	141	49	140	91	137	67
60–64	123	—	105	79	124	58	119	87	112	54	113	86	117	67
65–74	91	83	89	82	79	61	96	89	82	63	87	72	85	66
75+	62	72	75	75	63	53	72	71	78	71	67	60	65	58
Dispersion ratio[3]	2.3	—	2.1	1.1	2.5	1.1	1.9	1.2	1.8	0.7	2.1	1.5	2.1	1.2
Mean equivalent net income:														
Total 55+	100	91	100	90	100	70	100	87	100	77	100	80	100	77
55–59	121	—	134	83	140	70	126	100	124	64	124	96	120	74
60–64	116	—	101	92	121	74	114	95	109	69	110	91	111	78
65–74	98	96	93	91	84	72	97	93	89	75	93	83	93	80
75+	76	86	86	89	73	67	80	80	87	84	78	74	78	74
Dispersion ratio	1.6	—	1.6	0.9	1.9	1.0	1.6	1.3	1.4	0.8	1.5	1.3	1.5	1.0

1. The equivalent net income is measured by families.
2. The mean net incomes of the 'retired' families relative to the mean net income of all the elderly families (55+).
3. Dispersion ratio – the ratio of relative mean net income for the 75+ to 55–59 age group.
4. all – all elderly families
5. ret. – only 'retired' families

population of each elderly age group and of 'retired' elderly families by comparing their average income to the average of the total elderly population. The second examines the income distribution within each age group in terms of Gini coefficients and of the relative income shares of the different quintiles.[4] Two alternative measures of economic status will be presented, net income per family and equivalent net family income (i.e. net income adjusted for family size).

Relative mean incomes among age groups

Table 5.6 shows the relative mean net incomes for the different age groups in the various countries. The data are presented separately for all the elderly families and for 'retired' families only. The figures for all the elderly families show a similar pattern in all countries – relative mean net income declines as age increases. In Norway the steepest decline in the relative mean is from the 65–74 to the 75+ age group, whilst in West Germany it is from the 55–59 to the 60–64 age group. This is consistent with the fact that West Germany has a relatively high proportion of families in the 60–64 age group that have retired completely, whereas in Norway the effective retirement age is higher. In the other countries, the relative mean falls most sharply from the 60–64 to the 65–74 age group.

The relative mean net income of the 55–59 age group in the United Kingdom is the highest in the seven countries surveyed at 158. This is followed by West Germany and Norway with 156 and 144 respectively. The relative mean net income in the 75+ age group is lowest (62–63) in Norway and the United Kingdom and highest (78) in Israel. If the ratio of high to low relative mean net income within a country is taken as a crude measure of income dispersion or inequality among older age groups in that country, then the United Kingdom and Norway have the widest dispersion and Israel and Sweden have the narrowest.

A comparison of the 'retired' families with all the elderly families reveals that the net income of the 'retired' families in all age groups is lower, but the income dispersion among the four age groups within the 'retired' families is significantly smaller than that which was found in the general elderly population. This finding is particularly striking in West Germany, the United

Table 5.7 Bottom and top quintile income shares and Gini coefficient within each age group of family's head (based on net income per family)

Age of head		Norway	West Germany	United Kingdom	Sweden	Israel	United States	Canada
55–59	Bottom quintile	8.0	5.3	7.2	9.8	7.2	4.5	5.4
	Top quintile	34.3	46.8	38.5	32.1	38.9	39.5	38.8
	Gini coefficient	0.2672	0.4210	0.3166	0.2331	0.3227	0.3527	0.3369
60–64	Bottom quintile	7.2	5.2	6.1	10.1	6.3	3.0	4.5
	Top quintile	35.7	41.7	42.4	33.7	41.3	43.6	41.7
	Gini coefficient	0.2894	0.3573	0.3648	0.2475	0.3618	0.4118	0.3797
65–74	Bottom quintile	8.4	6.2	8.5	11.9	6.6	5.3	6.9
	Top quintile	38.9	42.0	43.2	32.3	45.4	44.6	43.9
	Gini coefficient	0.3069	0.3525	0.3418	0.2126	0.3881	0.3943	0.3686
75+	Bottom quintile	9.9	4.8	10.0	13.2	5.5	6.0	8.3
	Top quintile	37.7	41.0	43.2	30.5	52.6	47.0	44.2
	Gini coefficient	0.3069	0.3635	0.3183	0.1803	0.4671	0.4067	0.3564

Kingdom, Sweden and Canada. In these countries there are only small differences in the relative means of the first three age groups, and the decline in the relative mean of the 75+ age group is relatively moderate. The ratio of the highest to the lowest relative mean is about 1.1 in West Germany and the United Kingdom and 1.2 in Sweden and Canada.

In the United States, on the other hand, the data show a systematic decline in relative mean incomes among 'retired' age groups, so that the relative mean of the 75+ age group is only two-thirds that of the 55–59 age group. In Israel the pattern of the relative means of the 'retired' age groups is the opposite of that in the other countries: relative mean income rises with age so that the relative situation of older age groups is better than that of younger groups. This difference between Israel and the other countries stems from the fact that in Israel income from property is distributed most unequally among the various age groups in the 'retired' population. The relative mean property income of the 75+ age group is ten times as high as that of the youngest age group and double that of the 60–64 age group.

Table 5.7 also presents the relative mean net equivalent incomes, allowing an assessment of the impact of the adjustment of income for family size. The adjustment does not change the ranking of the countries by relative means and income dispersion among the age groups, but in all the countries it decreases the income gaps among the age groups. Moreover, the use of equivalent net income improves the situation of 'retired' families relative to all elderly families, indicating their generally smaller size.

Income distribution within age groups

Another important aspect of the distribution of income among elderly families is the distribution within each age group. Table 5.7 presents the Gini coefficients and the top and bottom quintile shares of family net income in each of the four age groups.[5] The data show that the patterns of change across the various age groups in the relative shares of the quintiles and in the Gini coefficients are not uniform in all the countries.

The distribution of income within each age group is more equal in Sweden than in the other countries. Norway occupies the

Table 5.8 Bottom and top quintile income shares and Gini coefficient within each age group of family's head (based on equivalent net income)

Age of head		Norway	West Germany	United Kingdom	Sweden	Israel	United States	Canada
55–59	Bottom quintile	9.9	7.4	9.7	10.7	7.5	5.9	7.8
	Top quintile	32.9	42.8	32.8	29.7	40.0	37.1	35.5
	Gini coefficient	0.2313	0.3539	0.2324	0.1942	0.3264	0.3143	0.2820
60–64	Bottom quintile	10.4	6.9	8.4	11.0	6.9	4.6	6.7
	Top quintile	32.6	36.1	35.5	30.0	43.0	39.6	37.7
	Gini coefficient	0.2259	0.2963	0.2803	0.1931	0.3573	0.3534	0.3136
65–74	Bottom quintile	10.5	7.1	10.9	14.1	7.7	6.6	8.7
	Top quintile	35.3	36.7	37.6	28.5	43.7	40.8	39.7
	Gini coefficient	0.2495	0.2981	0.2656	0.1426	0.3599	0.3416	0.3092
75+	Bottom quintile	11.4	5.6	12.0	15.1	7.4	7.0	10.0
	Top quintile	34.6	39.7	36.8	27.3	50.4	42.9	39.6
	Gini coefficient	0.2293	0.3395	0.2403	0.1258	0.4288	0.3554	0.291

second place and the United Kingdom is generally ranked third. This finding is shown in both the Gini coefficient and in the quintile shares: Sweden has the lowest Gini coefficient in each age group, the highest bottom quintile share and the lowest top quintile share. In West Germany, the distribution of income in the 55–59 age group is the least equal of all the countries, as is the case in the United States in the 60–64 and 65–74 age groups. In the oldest group inequality is greatest in Israel.

The differences between Sweden and the other countries, especially the United States and Israel, increase as one goes from the 55–59 age group to the oldest age group. In Sweden, the income of the top quintile in the 55–59 age group is 3.3 times as high as the income in the bottom quintile and the ratio falls to 2.3 in the 75+ age group. Moreover, the Gini coefficient in the 75+ age group is 30 per cent lower than in the 55–59 age group. On the other hand, in Israel, for example, the ratio of income in the top quintile to income in the bottom quintile rises from 5.4 in the 55–59 age group to 9.6 in the 75+ age group, and the Gini coefficient increases by about 45 per cent. The Gini coefficients in the 75+ age group in Israel and the United States are 2.5 and 2.3 times as high, respectively as in Sweden.

The characteristics of income distribution based on equivalent net income per person are presented in Table 5.8.[6] A comparison of these data with the data based on (unadjusted) net income per family shows that Gini coefficients calculated on the basis of equivalent net income per person are lower and that the lowest quintile share is greater while that of the highest quintile is smaller. This finding is true for all age groups in all countries. However, the patterns of change in inequality within each country as age increases broadly resemble those shown in the family net income distribution.

CONCLUSIONS

This chapter has examined the size of the retired population according to alternative definitions and studied a number of aspects of economic well-being within the elderly population in LIS countries. In particular, it highlighted the variations in well-being both within countries among the elderly in different age groups and between the relative position of the elderly in the different countries, and emphasised the role of transfer income in reducing inequality.

Among LIS countries public transfers and market income comprise different proportions of family gross income. The lowest relative share of transfer income is in Israel, the United States and Canada where market income still constitutes at least 50 per cent of the gross income of 'retired' families. Market income – earnings, property income and occupational pensions – is generally distributed less equally than public transfers. Therefore, one might expect to find a higher level of inequality in the income distribution in countries in which market income constitutes a relatively important component of gross income.

The data on the income composition of the elderly and on the Gini coefficients support, to a large extent, this hypothesis as applied to the elderly population. Except in the case of West Germany, the higher the relative share of market income, the more unequal is the income distribution within elderly families.

While the composition of average family income among the elderly is thus clearly an important factor in explaining cross-national variations in income inequality, the pattern is affected by other factors, not least of which is likely to be the distribution of transfer income among elderly families. Perhaps the most productive way forward in seeking explanations for cross-national variations in income inequality among the elderly, therefore, would be more detailed analyses of the relationships of such variations to the institutional characteristics which determine the distribution of transfer income in the various countries.

NOTES

1. In all the tables in this section, the countries appear in a descending order corresponding to their place according to the percentage of families in the 55+ age group among all families. Thus each table acquires an additional dimension alongside the variables presented in it.
2. No household of this type appears in Norway and Sweden because their surveys treat persons over 18 living with other adults as separate families (except that couples are treated as one family).
3. Direct taxes include income tax and the payroll taxes paid by

employees. The figure for Canada is affected by the absence of payroll taxes in the Canadian data.

4. The analyses in respect of West Germany are affected by the fact that 2.7 per cent of all families in West Germany are recorded as having zero incomes. The large majority of these families are elderly. The results presented in this paper do not adjust for this factor. Omitting these records or imputing an 'assigned income' would increase the share of the bottom quintile, decrease the poverty rates and might also change the relative mean incomes of the various elderly groups.

5. The families are ranked by family net income and each quintile includes 20 per cent of families.

6. The families are ranked by equivalent net income per person and each quintile includes 20 per cent of persons.

6 · ECONOMIC WELL-BEING AMONG ONE-PARENT FAMILIES

Richard Hauser and Ingo Fischer

INTRODUCTION

One-parent families are regarded as a growing social problem in many developed nations. In 1971 the XIIth Conference of European Ministers Responsible for Family Affairs chose it as the main theme of their conference. In 1974 the Finer Report investigated the situation in the United Kingdom and also made a thorough comparative study of several other European countries, namely Denmark, Norway, Sweden, the Netherlands and the Federal Republic of Germany (Finer, 1975). But the comparative part of the Finer Report was mainly restricted to the various institutional provisions for income maintenance of one-parent families, the administrative procedures and some complementary social services. Earnings and public transfers were compared only for a few standardised family types.

The Final Report of the Commission of the European Communities on the First Programme to Combat Poverty (European Community, 1981) showed on an empirical basis that one-parent families bear a very high risk of becoming poor, especially if they have two or more children. In 1982 a sequel to this study dealt especially with the situation of one-parent families in EC member countries. (Frijs *et al.*, 1982). It concluded that in most member countries the empirical information about these families is insufficient to make precise comparisons, but it confirmed that these groups bear a poverty risk far above average.

Another comparative study by Kahn and Kamerman (1983) reinvestigated the institutional provisions for families with children – among them one-parent families – in eight developed countries (the six countries examined in this chapter plus Australia and France); it went further in that it distinguished 15 family types and compared their relative positions using the statutory provisions in each country for calculating the specific benefits. Only within-country comparisons of various family types were produced and no attempt was made to provide between-country comparisons of absolute standards of living. This study left several questions unanswered:

1. The empirical frequency of each family type within each country.
2. The relative economic position of each family type within each country.
3. The influence of factor incomes, and of private and public transfers on the relative economic position of each family type in each country.
4. The relative living standards of each family type emerging from between-country comparisons.

The LIS database is suited to deal with these questions. An exploratory analysis of one-parent families, restricted to questions 1–3, will be presented in this chapter. Between-country comparisons of living standards bring up a host of additional methodological problems and, therefore, no attempt is made to deal with the fourth question.

The countries selected are those for which sets of individual cross-section data are incorporated into the LIS database; namely the United States, Canada, the United Kingdom, Sweden, Israel and West Germany. (Although data for Norway are integrated into the LIS database, this country is left out of the work presented in this chapter because the data are not suited to distinguish one-parent families according to the same criteria that were used for other countries.)

THE RELATIVE ECONOMIC POSITIONS OF ONE-PARENT FAMILIES WITH MINOR CHILDREN

The framework of comparison

The living conditions of one-parent families can be compared to several other groups within each country. Single persons or couples without children or two-parent families with minor children are the most obvious reference groups. But one could also compare them to all households with a head of household of working age or all households with a head aged 20–45. For this analysis we have chosen two-parent families with minor children as the reference group in order to concentrate on the differences between family types with minor children. This means that the differences between countries in the relative positions of families with minor children compared to singles or to couples without children, either at working age or at pensionable age, are not taken into account. These relative positions of all families with minor children may vary from country to country for many reasons, one of the most important being differences in tax policies and social security provisions with respect to the elderly and to single persons and couples without children.

Compared to two-parent families, one-parent families with minor children are disadvantaged in many aspects. The lone parent has to raise the children without being able to share the duties of nursing, day care, education and providing a home with a second parent. In case of sickness, accident or other emergency, no spouse is available to help out. Thus, an elementary form of risk-sharing is missing.

The single parent also has to maintain by her or himself the integration of the family into the social network of relatives, friends, neighbourhood and community, and to provide opportunities for the integration of the children. Finally, the lone parent has to be the sole breadwinner, if the family is not fully supported in cash or kind by private or public transfers.

A comparison between one-parent and two-parent families with respect to all economic, social and psychological aspects of their living conditions within the framework of a comparative six-country study is not feasible at present. Therefore, a pragmatic reduction of the dimensions of comparison is necessary.

Three important economic dimensions of living conditions of families with children are net income, the availability of time for child care and the availability of in-kind public transfers.[1]

If a lone parent works full time, there is less time left for child care and household duties than in a two-parent family with both spouses in full-time employment. This has to be considered as an unfavourable element of the living conditions. The difference in available time is even more disadvantageous to the working lone parent when compared with the two-parent family where one spouse can spend all his/her time in child rearing and household duties. Only if a single parent does not need to spend time earning an income may the balance of available time be in his/her favour.

Therefore, a comparison of the positions of one-parent and two-parent families in principle ought to account for these differences in available time by using the wider concept of economic resources instead of net income only.

To a limited extent personal child care by parents can be substituted, by public or private services from outside the family, usually at a cost, e.g. day care centres, boarding schools. These differences also ought to be taken into account in calculating the relative position of one-parent families. Similarly there may exist differences between one-parent and two-parent families with respect to the availability of in-kind public transfers, especially in the areas of health care, housing, public transportation and education. Since these differences are not revealed in net incomes, modifications would be necessary.

At present it is not possible to account systematically and comprehensively for differences concerning available time, the use of services from outside the family and the availability of in-kind public transfers. Thus there are limitations in the comparisons, based only on net income, which follow.

Various theoretical concepts of one-parent and two-parent families exist, depending on the problem an analyst wants to tackle. With a legally oriented approach, institutional characteristics like marriage, blood relations and liabilities for maintenance are used to define families. A more functional approach emphasises factual relations between persons, like cohabitation, income sharing and exchange of personal services within a household.

Table 6.1 One-parent families[1], two-parent families[2] and other units in six industrialised countries

Country (year)	One-parent families				Two-parent families				Other units				All			
	Family no.[5] %[6]		Persons no. %		Family no. %		Persons no. %		Family no %		Persons no. %		Family no. %		Persons no. %	
Sweden (1979)	0.192	4.4	0.467	5.7	0.887	20.3	3.355	41.0	3.285	75.3	4.364	53.3	4.364	100	8.186	100
United Kingdom[3] (1979)	0.228	3.3	0.640	3.5	2.035	29.5	8.141	44.5	4.625	67.2	9.529	52.0	6.888	100	18.310	100
Israel[4] (1979)	0.013	1.5	0.037	1.2	0.346	38.7	1.536	50.1	0.534	59.8	1.493	48.7	0.893	100	3.066	100
United States (1979)	5.061	6.1	14.803	6.8	20.867	24.7	83.159	38.2	58.055	69.2	119.731	55.0	83.983	100	217.693	100
Canada (1981)	0.383	4.3	1.031	4.3	2.490	27.8	9.881	41.6	6.081	67.9	12.852	54.1	8.954	100	23.764	100
West Germany (1981)	0.576	2.5	1.444	2.7	5.472	24.0	20.369	37.4	16.795	73.5	32.598	59.9	22.843	100	54.411	100

1. One adult living with one or more minor children (under 18) in his/her own household with no other adults present.
2. Two adults (e.g. married couple, mother and daughter) living with one or more minor children (under 18) in their household with no other adults present.
3. UK data are actual number of person or family records, not millions of persons.
4. Israeli figures for urban population only.
5. Millions of units.
6. Percentage of all units.

Given the differences in the legal systems among countries, a functional approach seems to be preferable for comparative studies. Following this line, an adult caring for one or more minor children (under 18), without another adult being present in the household, is considered to be a one-parent family. This definition includes a natural parent living with his/her own children, but also adopted children or foster children. For various reasons, one-parent families sometimes live together in the same household with other adults, like their parents or relatives or unrelated persons. These living arrangements may result in sharing household costs and in the exchange of personal services that are beneficial for all household members. Since the intra-household transfers are not known, we concentrate our analysis on the one-parent families with minor children who live in a household of their own. This definition is narrower than definitions in official statistics, thus decreasing the proportion of one-parent families to be found in the datasets.

According to this functional approach, two-parent families were defined as husband and wife, living with minor children in the same household with no other adults present, or two adults living with minor children in the same household.[2] To bring out differences between one-parent and two-parent families more clearly, families with more than two adults are classified among 'other units', as are single persons and other household types.

The analysis is based upon net income or elements thereof. Net income is defined as factor income plus employment-related pensions plus public and private transfers, minus direct taxes and payroll taxes. Mean values of net income will be defined alternatively as net income per family, net income per capita or net equivalent income per capita, following the procedure outlined in Chapter 1. Between-country comparisons refer only to relative positions within countries, thus avoiding comparisons of absolute levels of living standards of various groups.

Empirical results: demographic aspects

The analysis begins by presenting some demographic information, based on the LIS data tapes. Table 6.1 shows total numbers and proportions of one-parent and two-parent families in all the countries. The proportions of one-parent families in relation to all units vary from 1.5 per cent (Israel) to 6.1 per cent (United States) with a lower middle group comprising West Germany (2.5 per cent) and the United Kingdom (3.3 per cent) and an upper middle group consisting of Canada (4.3 per cent) and Sweden (4.4 per cent).

Compared with the calculations in Chapter 3 these figures are lower for all countries, except Sweden. This is the result of three effects. First, only one-parent families living in a household of their own were counted, which reduces the number of one-parent families considerably. Second, the upper age limit of 65 for the parent was not used, which might result in a slight increase. Third, the analysis was not restricted to natural parents, but included all adults living with children in their household. This also increases the number of one-parent families, but clearly the first effect dominates the other two. Similar effects explain the lower percentages of two-parent families in all countries, except Sweden.

An examination of the ratios of one-parent to two-parent families produces a ranking of countries in which the top group consists of the United States (24.7 per cent) and Sweden (21.8 per cent). Israel has the lowest ratio of 3.9 per cent and the other countries are in-between (West Germany 10.4 per cent; the United Kingdom 11.2 per cent; Canada 15.5 per cent). These ratios roughly correspond to information from other sources, for example Millar (1985), if the more narrow definitions in this analysis are taken into account.

The figures show considerable variation in the demographic composition of the populations. These discrepancies have to be kept in mind in evaluating the results of the following section which presents the relative economic positions of one-parent families, since it clearly makes a difference whether an unfavourable relative position concerns only a small or a large proportion of all families with children.

Empirical results: relative economic position

The relative economic position of one group in relation to another group, as measured by the group averages of net incomes, can be considered as a rough overall measure of an important aspect of the living conditions of these groups. Since household size, household economies and differences in structure of need among members ought to be taken into account, net income per adult equivalent unit (or economic welfare position), is preferable to net income per family or net income per capita for a comparison. Table 6.2 presents the results for the six countries selected.

As might be expected, the economic welfare position of one-parent families in all six countries is worse than that of two-parent families by all measures of average net income. Although the mean ratios are different depending on the kind of averages used, the ranking of the countries is practically the same. Concentrating on the relative welfare positions shows that Sweden is in a top position, meaning that the discrepancy between one-parent and two-parent families is rather small (13 per cent). A middle group consists of West Germany, the United Kingdom and Israel with a discrepancy of a little more than 20 per cent. In Canada the welfare position of one-parent families is on average about 34 per cent below that of two-parent families, and in the United States the discrepancy is a high 43 per cent.

Relating these results to demographic patterns, it appears that on the one hand Sweden, despite a rather high proportion of one-parent families, has managed to keep them fairly close to the two-parent families, while on the other hand in the United

Table 6.2 Ranking of countries according to relative positions of one-parent families compared to two-parent families using average net incomes

Country	Net income per family		Net income per capita		Welfare position	
	Rank	Mean ratio	Rank	Mean Ratio	Rank	Mean ratio
Sweden	1	0.63	1	0.97	1	0.87
West Germany	2	0.59	2	0.87	2	0.78
United Kingdom	3	0.58	4	0.83	4	0.76
Israel	4	(0.57)[1]	2	(0.87)[1]	2	(0.78)[1]
Canada	5	0.49	5	0.73	5	0.66
United States	6	0.45	6	0.62	6	0.57

1. Derived from less than 20 households in the sample.

States – the country under review with the highest proportion of one-parent families – they fall far behind the two-parent families.

These overall results give rise to a number of questions that will be dealt with in the following sections.

DETERMINANTS OF RELATIVE ECONOMIC POSITIONS

On an intermediate level of analysis, differences in the relative economic positions of one-parent families compared to two-parent families are a result of differences in the following:

1. Factor income.
2. Private transfers received.
3. Public transfers received.
4. Taxes and social security contributions paid.
5. Household size, if income per capita or per adult equivalent unit is used for comparison.

These intermediate level determinants can in principle be related to differences in more basic causal factors specific to each country, but the limitations of the database prevent a full causal analysis. The focus is mainly on explaining the ranking of the countries as determined by the relative welfare positions of one-parent families.

Factor incomes and labour force participation

Factor incomes consist of three broad categories:

1. Wages and salaries.
2. Self-employment income.
3. Cash property income.

Of these categories, earnings are by far the dominant income source for the average family. Although information about the families' factor incomes in the various countries is used, the analysis of its determinants is concentrated on earnings since no information about causal factors determining differences with respect to property income is available.

The earnings of a family depend upon its potential earnings capacity and the actual utilisation of this capacity. The earnings capacity of a family can be measured by hours of work time available multiplied by the wage rate that corresponds with the qualifications and other labour market characteristics of the potential labour supplier. But the time necessary for the upbringing of children ('upbringing capacity') competes with earnings capacity for the total available time of the adults of a family.

The economic position of two-parent families is based upon the earnings capacity of at least one breadwinner. If household duties and child care obligations are shared by both spouses, both may be able to earn an individual income, even if the second breadwinner does so on a part-time basis. On the other hand the adult in a one-parent family can only take on a full-time job if the circumstances are very favourable. Availability of full-time child care facilities is most crucial. On an average, the earnings capacity of one-parent families can be expected to be lower.[3] Since differences in earnings capacity between one-parent and two-parent families are likely to be the basic factor in all countries under review, it is expected that the relative economic position of one-parent families compared to two-parent families – based on factor income – will be less favourable everywhere.

The utilisation of earnings capacity by those actually working depends – among other factors – upon the availability of other income (e.g. private and public transfers), the availability of jobs, and the wage rate, net of taxes and contributions. Differences between one-parent and two-parent families on the one hand and differences between these factors among the various countries on the other will consequently modify the results.

Differences in earnings capacity and in the utilisation of earnings capacity among countries show up in both overall and in specific labour force participation rates. Since one-parent families are mostly headed by women, female labour force participation rates are of special significance. Depending on the cultural background, the educational opportunities and the availability of jobs for women, the overall female labour force participation rates differ among countries. A high overall female labour force participation rate will indicate higher earnings both of one-parent and two-parent families. The effect on the relative position of one-parent families compared with two-parent families is, thus, not unequivocal. For example, it may be that the better job opportunities for women can be used more easily by women of two-parent families because they possess a larger range of alternatives in rearranging their household and child care responsibilities. If this were the case, the relative economic position of one-parent families (as measured by factor income) would be less favourable in countries with a higher overall female labour force participation rate. This influence, however, can be counteracted by other effects.

Apart from this, if one considers the specific female labour force participation rates of the female heads of one-parent families, it can be expected that the relative position of one-parent families – based upon factor income – will be better the higher the specific female labour force participation rate. This effect can be modified if there are differences in the average working time of the female heads of one-parent families, e.g. if in one of these countries a high single-mother labour force participation rate is based mainly on part-time work, while in another country, with a similar participation rate, full-time jobs are the norm.

Given a majority of female-headed one-parent families, additional differences among countries in the relative factor income positions of one-parent families can be expected if the wage rate differentials between the breadwinners of both family types differ. Such wage rate differentials can be found if the following exist:

1. Wage discrimination against women in particular jobs.
2. Jobs available for women are concentrated in low wage industries or sectors.
3. Women, on average, show lower levels of qualification owing to lower education, lower vocational training levels or shorter periods of work experience.
4. There are fewer career opportunities for women in general or for those seeking part-time jobs.
5. Female heads of one-parent families seeking work on an average are younger than male breadwinners of two-parent families and thus have shorter periods of work experience.
6. There are higher unemployment rates for women in general or for those seeking part-time jobs.

The influence of differences in wage differentials on the relative economic positions of one-parent families is additionally modified if the proportions of one-parent families headed by women differ considerably among countries.

At present, it is not possible to disentangle fully the various determinants of intercountry differences. Merely a few elements can be highlighted.

Table 6.3 shows the average factor incomes of one-parent and two-parent families in relation to overall average factor income (except in Sweden). The ratio between one-parent and two-parent families is highest for West Germany and lowest for Israel, with the United Kingdom being close to Israel, with the United States and Canada in-between. This result is consistent with the basic hypothesis that the earnings capacity of one-parent families is considerably smaller than that of two-parent families, notwithstanding the various additional factors which have a modifying influence. In addition the discrepancy between one-parent and two-parent families is so large that it would not disappear if averages per adult equivalent unit were used instead of averages per family.

An examination of overall male and female labour force participation rates and of the rates for heads of one-parent families (Table 6.4) indicates that the one-parent rates are generally higher than the overall rates (except the male one-

Table 6.3 Ratio of average factor income of family types to overall average factor income per unit (except Sweden[1])

Country	One-parent families	Two-parent families	Other units	All units	One-parent family/Two parent family Ratio	Rank
West Germany	64	148	86	100	43	1
Canada	46	127	92	100	36	2
United States	43	134	93	100	32	3
United Kingdom	36	133	89	100	27	4
Israel	(29)[2]	132	81	100	22	5

1. Sweden is excluded because calculations were not possible within the first round of calculations.
2. Derived from less than 20 households in the sample.

Table 6.4 Labour force participation rates

Country	Male					Female				
	Overall rate[1]		One-parent rate[2]		Relative difference	Overall rate		One-parent rate		Relative difference
	%	Rank	%	Rank	%	%	Rank	%	Rank	%
West Germany (1981)	80.6	4	84.0	3	+4.2	49.6	4	74.8	1	+50.8
Canada (1981)	86.4	2	94.1	1	+8.9	58.9	1	68.5	3	+16.3
United States (1979)	85.7	3	93.9	2	+9.6	58.9	1	72.6	2	+23.3
United Kingdom (1979)	90.7	1	71.4	4	−21.3	58.2	3	66.5	4	+14.3
Sweden (1979)	87.9		95.3		+8.4	72.9		92.4		+26.7
Israel (1979)	—[3]		(100.0)[4]		—[3]	—[3]		(63.6)[4]		—[3]

1. Overall labour force participation rate is defined as total labour force divided by population of working age (15–64) at mid-year. Source: OECD. Employment Outlook, Paris, 1983.
2. One-parent labour force participation rate is defined as one-parent families with earnings divided by all one-parent families of the same sex.
3. No figures available.
4. Derived from less than 20 households in the sample.

parent rate for the United Kingdom), indicating the economic pressure for one-parent families to utilise available earnings capacity. Also the male one-parent rates generally are higher than the female ones. However, apart from the United States, the relative differences among overall and one-parent female rates are larger than those for male rates.

In the case of West Germany, both the low female overall rate as well as the high female one-parent rate are consistent with West Germany having the highest ratio of one-parent factor incomes; the reverse consistency is true for the United Kingdom. The middle position of the United States and Canada is also consistent.

Some additional information can be gained by looking at Table 6.5, which shows the proportions of male- and female-headed one-parent families and, among those with earnings, the sub-groups with full-time and part-time jobs. Assuming that female wage rates are, on average, lower than male wage rates, the high proportion of male-headed one-parent families in West Germany, most of them with a full-time job, also explains part of the high relative factor income of single parents in that country.

Among female-headed one-parent families, the proportion of lone parents with earnings is also highest in West Germany and lowest in Israel and the United Kingdom, with the United States and Canada in-between (compare Table 6.4), but with more than half of female heads working full-time in West Germany and in Canada and less than half in the other countries. These higher proportions of full-time working female heads may also contribute to the relatively higher single-parent factor incomes in West Germany and Canada.

Although results along the lines of Table 6.3 could not be calculated for Sweden, the results of Tables 6.4 and 6.5 give reason to expect this country also to be in the top group with respect to the ratio of earnings of one-parent to two-parent families. This section consequently can be concluded with the finding that one-parent families in Sweden and West Germany are strongly work-oriented while in the United Kingdom and Israel work orientation is considerably weaker, with Canada and the United States taking a middle position.

Table 6.5 Earnings and working time of one-parent families by sex of head of household

Earnings and working time by country	Male	Female	All[2]
West Germany			
All	29.34	70.66	100.00
No earnings	4.69	(17.71)[1]	22.40
With earnings	24.65	52.95	77.60
Full time	16.49	28.99	45.48
Part time	8.33	23.90	32.22
Canada			
All	13.28	86.72	100.00
No earnings	(0.78)[1]	27.34	28.12
With earnings	12.50	59.38	71.88
Full time	9.38	36.53	44.30
Part time	(3.13)[1]	27.12	30.97
United States			
All	12.37	87.63	100.00
No earnings	0.75	23.97	24.72
With earnings	11.62	63.66	75.28
Full time	7.77	36.53	44.30
Part time	3.85	27.12	30.97
United Kingdom			
All	12.28	87.72	100.00
No earnings	(3.51)[1]	29.39	32.90
With earnings	8.77	58.33	67.10
Full time	(7.46)[1]	25.00	32.46
Part time	(1.32)[1]	33.33	34.65
Israel			
All	(8.33)[1]	(91.66)[1]	100.00
No earnings	—	(33.33)[1]	(33.33)[1]
With earnings	(8.33)[1]	(58.33)[1]	(66.67)[1]
Full time	(8.33)[1]	(8.33)[1]	(16.66)[1]
Part time	—	(50.00)[1]	(50.00)[1]
Sweden			
All	10.94	89.06	100.00
No earnings	(0.52)[1]	6.77	7.29
With earnings	10.42	82.29	92.71
Full time	8.33	35.94	44.27
Part time	(2.09)[1]	46.35	48.44

1. Derived from less than 20 households in the sample.
2. Lines and rows may not exactly add up due to rounding errors.

Private transfers

Private transfers in favour of one-parent families can be a substitute for earned income. Apart from private transfers which are based upon legal obligations of maintenance, there may also exist voluntary transfers. However, these two types cannot be distinguished in these data.

Since maintenance liabilities differ in most countries with respect to the marital status of the parent who is head of household, at least seven types of (standard) one-parent families can be distinguished:

a1) Head of household never married and second parent still alive and known.

a2) Head of household never married and second parent deceased or without sufficient income or unknown.[4]

b) Head of household widowed.

c1) Head of household divorced and former spouse still alive and known.

c2) Head of household divorced and former spouse deceased or without sufficient income or unknown.

d1) Head of household permanently separated and spouse still alive and known.

d2) Head of household permanently separated and spouse without sufficient income or unknown.

If a parent has married several times, additional types could be distinguished. However, these cases are ignored, as are those of non-standard one-parent families (e.g. adults with a foster child).

Without presenting a detailed analysis of the legal regulations for all of these countries (see Max Planck Institut, 1983), it is likely that only those in categories c1 and d1 will usually be receiving maintenance for both the parent and the child(ren), while category a1 may be entitled to maintenance for the child(ren). Therefore only types c1 and d1 might receive private maintenance payments sufficient for a living standard comparable to a two-parent family, provided that the maintenance liabilities are actually fulfilled by the absent parent. This means that the following ranking of one-parent families might be expected if the ranking is only based on income from private transfers:

1. Types c1 and d1.
2. Type a1.
3. Types a2, b, c2, d2.

Differences among countries, with respect to the same type of one-parent families, might depend upon the following:

1. Different legal regulations for both kinds of maintenance payments with respect to the preconditions, the amount and the duration of the payments.
2. The income of persons who are liable to pay maintenance.
3. The actual degree to which maintenance liabilities are fulfilled, which may in turn depend on the sanctions imposed by law for not fulfilling these obligations.
4. Since legal obligations for private transfers in favour of two-parent families only exist in exceptional cases,[5] we can expect that private transfers are far more significant for one-parent families than for two-parent families. This expectation is supported by the results of Table 6.6.

Although there are also a few private transfers in favour of a small proportion of two-parent families and other units, the average amount going to one-parent families is a high multiple of the overall average. If the composition of the group of one-parent families – according to the types mentioned above – were similar in each country, the results of Table 6.6 would indicate that the fulfilment of maintenance obligations on the one hand and the amounts paid on the other are much more favourable for one-parent families in West Germany and in the United Kingdom than they are in the United States and in Israel. However, it could also be possible that the differences between the two groups of countries result from a far higher proportion

Table 6.6 Ratio of average private transfers received by family types to overall average private transfers per unit (except Sweden and Canada[1])

Country	One-parent families	Two-parent families	Other units	All units
West Germany	1437	80	61	100
United States	594	104	56	100
United Kingdom	1382	50	59	100
Israel	(282)[2]	105	92	100

1. For Sweden and Canada no information available.
2. Derived from less than 20 households in the sample.

of one-parent families without any maintenance claims in the United States and in Israel. Unfortunately, the LIS database does not allow for all countries a clear distinction among lone parents who are either never married, or separated, divorced or widowed. Consequently, a more detailed analysis is precluded. Tentative results for West Germany show a ranking of one-parent family types with parents 'separated' ranking top, followed by 'divorced', 'never married' and 'widowed', as was to be expected.

The significance of private transfers for one-parent families in relation to other income types is also further revealed by Table 6.7 below.

Public transfers

Cash public transfers in favour of one-parent as well as two-parent families are a significant element of these families' economic position in each country. Differences among the relative economic positions of one-parent families are partly due to differences in the public transfer systems of the various countries.

Among public transfers in favour of families, three types can be distinguished according to their main purpose.

First, there are public transfers to substitute for private maintenance obligations. Here several sub-types can be found:

1. Transfers in favour of children whose second parent is alive, but who does not fulfil his/her maintenance obligation.
2. Survivor's benefits to widows/widowers or to orphans.
3. Transfers in favour of the lone parent (other than survivor's benefit) whose claim to maintenance is not fulfilled or who has no maintenance claim and who is not able to or not supposed to earn a full income through work.

Such benefits may be tax-financed and either means tested or universal, or they may be social insurance benefits based on former contributions. Where such benefits exist, obviously the relative economic position of one-parent families is improved, with the magnitude of this improvement depending on the level of benefits.

Second, there are public transfers to reduce the costs of children to all families. These transfers can either be universal for all children without any means test or they can be subject to means tests. They may be restricted to children of higher order of birth or they may increase with the number of children in the family. There can be additional programmes to support children in higher education. Usually these transfers are tax-financed.

Although these benefits equally improve the economic position of one-parent as well as of two-parent families, one-parent families who – on average – have lower factor incomes gain relatively more and consequently improve their relative position. It can be expected that in countries with generous transfers of this type the relative economic position of one-parent families is more favourable.

Third, there may be public transfers to secure a minimum income either for all members of society, or for certain groups, among whom one-parent families may be included. These transfers usually are social assistance schemes, which are means tested and usually financed by taxes.

Since the income of one-parent families from other sources is often very low, the relative economic position of one-parent families tends to be more favourable in countries with generous social assistance levels.

The main characteristics of each of these three categories of the public transfer systems as they apply to one-parent families in the various countries studied in this chapter are summarised in the following paragraphs.[6]

Benefits to substitute for the earnings of persons leaving work to care for their children, to substitute for private maintenance liabilities which are not fulfilled, or to cover income loss due to maternity did not develop until recent decades. Maternity allowances exist in the United Kingdom, Sweden, West Germany and Israel. In Israel and the United Kingdom each mother receives a small grant at the time this data is collected, while in Sweden and West Germany only working mothers on maternity leave receive benefits. Sweden has the most generous plan (Parental Insurance), enabling both parents to participate in various forms of paid and unpaid partial job leave.

The special situation of one-parent families is recognised in different ways in four of the countries. The United Kingdom grants an extra child allowance to these families. Sweden, Israel and West Germany have established a new benefit, the Advance Maintenance Allowance, which under certain conditions is repayable by the liable absent parent.

Transfers to compensate for income loss due to the death of the breadwinner can be considered as 'old' benefits which have a long tradition. Survivor's benefits exist in all countries, although benefits for younger widows/widowers and orphans are sometimes very meagre or non-existent.

Universal benefits to meet part of the costs for small children and educational benefits for older children (and young adults as well) exist in five of the six countries. The United Kingdom, West Germany, Israel and Sweden grant each family with minor children a universal child allowance which is not means tested. Sometimes the amount per child increases with the number of children. Canada's Family Allowance Plan includes child benefits which vary from district to district. Educational benefits and programmes for free school meals or reduced rates for means-tested day care centres can be found in the United Kingdom, West Germany, Sweden and Israel. Means-tested student grants for adult students are available in the United Kingdom, West Germany and Sweden.

Each country has a social assistance scheme, securing a minimum income either for the whole population or at least for certain groups, although such a minimum may be below any acknowledged poverty line. The United Kingdom, West Germany, Canada and Israel apply common rules nationwide, whereas in the United States and Sweden, different rules are applied by state, district or local authorities. As far as the United States is concerned, only the means-tested Food Stamp programme applies the same rules nationwide. Special arrangements for providing a minimum for particular sub-groups can be found in the United States, the United Kingdom and in Canada. Aid to Families with Dependent Children in the United States is a state-level means-tested programme, focused on one-parent families and, in some states, families with an unemployed father as well. In the United Kingdom the Family Income Supplement is a means-tested programme, directed only to families with an adult working full-time. Canada's Family Allowance Programme also provides means-tested benefits for low income families which take the form of a refundable tax credit.

These functionally defined categories or public transfers could not completely be reproduced with the available LIS data. Hence, transfers are divided into social insurance transfers, means-tested

Table 6.7 Market income, monetary public and private transfers and taxes as percentage of average gross income by family type

Country Type of family	Market income and other cash income 1	Monetary public transfers				Private transfers 6	Taxes 7
		Social insurance transfers (except child and family allowances) 2	Means-tested income 3	Child and family allowances 4	All public transfers 5		
Sweden							
Two-parent family	—	—	—	—	—	—	—
One-parent family	63.4	15.3	16.6	4.7	36.6	—	21.3
Other units	—	—	—	—	—	—	—
West Germany							
Two-parent family	94.3	2.1	0.2	3.3	5.6	0.1	27.2
One-parent family	78.2	10.3	2.3	4.3	16.9	4.9	21.2
Other units	78.4	20.2	0.7	0.5	21.4	0.2	20.4

United Kingdom							
Two-parent famiy	86.3	7.2	1.4	4.7	13.3	0.4	16.9
One-parent family	45.4	7.1	16.5	8.5	32.1	22.5	7.2
Other units	80.4	16.4	2.0	0.5	18.9	0.7	17.2
Israel							
Two-parent family	93.6	1.1	0.3	4.1	5.5	0.9	32.6
One-parent family	$(47.7)^2$	$(33.5)^2$	$(5.7)^2$	$(7.6)^2$	$(46.8)^2$	$(5.5)^2$	$(10.9)^2$
Other units	88.4	8.7	0.4	1.4	10.5	1.1	25.2
Canada							
Two-parent family	94.2	2.5	1.4	1.9	5.8	—	16.5
One-parent family	79.7	4.6	12.1	3.6	20.3	—	10.8
Other units	89.7	8.9	1.1	0.3	10.3	—	14.7
United States							
Two-parent family	96.8	1.8	0.9	—	2.7	0.5	21.6
One-parent family	76.9	2.1	14.3	—	16.4	6.7	12.9
Other units	89.6	9.3	0.8	—	10.1	0.3	21.0

1. No figures available owing to technical reasons.
2. Derived from less than 20 households in the sample.

transfers and child family allowances. Table 6.7 presents the results as percentages of average gross income for three family types.

Column 1 presents similar information as Table 6.3, but from a different perspective. The ratio of market income and other cash income between one-parent and two-parent families is rather high in West Germany, Canada and the United States (and presumably Sweden), while it is much lower for the United Kingdom and Israel.

Focusing on the percentages of all cash public transfers (column 5), two groups are revealed: Israel, the United Kingdom and Sweden rely heavily upon public transfers for their one-parent families, while in Canada, West Germany and the United States these percentages are only roughly one half of those of the other groups. Consequently the top rank of Sweden with respect to the relative welfare position of one-parent families is mainly explained by high public transfers in combination with high labour force participation. The medium rank of the United Kingdom and Israel is mostly due to high public transfers (and very high private transfers in the United Kingdom). West Germany's second rank depends much more upon high labour force participation than upon generous public transfers. The bottom ranks of Canada and the United States are the result of medium ranks with market incomes, but rather low public transfers.

With the exception of West Germany, the percentages of public transfers are highest for one-parent families, showing a considerable public concern towards these groups. West Germany's public concern seems to be more towards pensioners who are the largest group among 'other units'.

Looking at the structure of cash public transfers in favour of one-parent families (columns 2, 3 and 4), Table 6.7 indicates a strong reliance on means-tested benefits in Canada and in the United States, a balance between means-tested and non-means-tested benefits in the United Kingdom and Sweden, and a clear dominance of social insurance benefits in Israel and West Germany. The strong reliance on means-tested benefits (presumably with low income limits) and the absence of universal child allowances in the United States might contribute to the unfavourable relative welfare position of one-parent families in Canada and in the United States.

Income taxes, payroll taxes and social security contributions

Income taxes, payroll taxes and social security contributions can be considered as negative monetary transfers which influence net income and thus the welfare positions of family types. Preferential tax treatment of one-parent families compared to two-parent families results in implicit transfers which contribute favourably to the relative welfare position of one-parent families. Implicit transfers can partly be a substitute for explicit public transfers. Therefore, both types have to be taken into account since some countries rely more than others on implicit transfers, especially with respect to children. The definition of the reference tax regulations (without any implicit transfers and without any preferential treatment), is, however, difficult and means that differences in implicit transfers between countries cannot be separately measured, even though they are an influence on net income levels.

As can be seen from column 7 of Table 6.7, the percentages of taxes and contributions of one-parent families are somewhat lower in all countries. This fact could be a result of one or more of the following factors: lower average factor incomes, preferential treatment of one-parent families in the tax system, non-taxability of some components of gross income (for instance, public or private transfers) or from exemption of certain types of income from social security contributions. Differing institutional regulations in the various countries additionally contribute to the intercountry differences in percentages.

DISTRIBUTIONAL ASPECTS

Up to now, the economic status of one-parent families has only been discussed by using relative positions, based upon group averages. The LIS database enables the supplementation of this analysis by some distributional information for five countries. Israel has to be excluded because the group of one-parent families contained in the sample is too small to be disaggregated much further. The analysis will again be restricted to comparing one-parent and two-parent families in each country by their welfare positions, using net income per adult equivalent unit as a welfare measure.

Based upon *a priori* reasoning very little can be said about the distribution of one-parent and two-parent families, because the main determinants (labour force participation, private transfers, public transfers and taxes) influence families on each income level in a different way. These interrelationships do not lend themselves easily to generalisation. The only immediate hypothesis is based upon differences in earnings capacity in the needs of various family types, and upon the general conclusion which follows from the discussion of the public transfer systems, that public transfers do not fully compensate for any reductions of earnings capacity and for increases in need with an increasing family size. Thus the percentages of one-parent and two-parent families which are below the average welfare position may be expected to increase with family size. Additionally this increase may be expected to be greater for one-parent families than for two-parent families because of the greater reduction in earnings capacity.

The analysis will focus on the question of whether the ranking of countries with respect to the inequality of welfare positions among their one-parent and two-parent families differs from their ranking by the relative economic positions of one-parent families. The countries, therefore, are ranked in the following tables according to the relative position of one-parent families, as in Table 6.2. Ranks according to inequality measures are given separately.

Table 6.8 presents Gini coefficients as an overall measure of inequality. Regarding the inequality among one-parent families, the ranking of the five countries is almost equal to the relative welfare positions, the only exception being the exchange between the United Kingdom and West Germany. The discrepancy between the least unequal (Sweden) and the most unequal (United States) is very large considering the generally low sensitivity of Gini coefficients. With respect to two-parent families, the whole middle group changes its ranks, but the discrepancy between the top and the bottom position is much smaller. Except for Sweden, the inequality among one-parent families is considerably greater than among two-parent families.

Judging by these results, Sweden succeeds in securing a high relative position for its one-parent families and also in reducing inequality within both family types to a large extent. West Germany can secure a rather high relative position for its one-

Table 6.8 Gini-coefficients[1] of the welfare positions of persons in one-parent and two-parent families for five countries (except Israel[2])

Country	One-parent families		Two-parent families	
	Gini	Rank	Gini	Rank
Sweden	0.175	1	0.181	1
West Germany[3]	0.345	3	0.269	4
United Kingdom	0.290	2	0.229	2
Canada	0.366	4	0.259	3
United States	0.383	5	0.273	5

1. Gini coefficients were calculated on a person basis: each person was assigned the welfare position of its family derived from the family's net income per adult equivalent unit.
2. Countries implicitly ranked according to the relative welfare positions of one-parent families as in Table 6.2.
3. The results for West Germany are based on a sample that contains one-parent families and two-parent families which did not reveal their net income: the Gini coefficients, therefore, are slightly biased upwards.

parent families but combines this with much greater inequality among its one-parent and two-parent families. The United Kingdom reduces inequality within both family types considerably, but to a larger extent for two-parent families. It merely secures a middle rank for the relative position of its one-parent families. Canada and the United States reveal rather low relative positions as well as considerable inequality, especially for their one-parent families.

As is well known, using Gini coefficients alone gives an imperfect measure of inequality; they thus need to be supplemented by additional information. Table 6.9 presents results about the distribution of economic welfare measure by quintiles of persons living either in one-parent or in two-parent families. An examination of the share of welfare among persons from one-parent families in the bottom and top quintiles confirms the ranking by Gini coefficients. Considering the small differences between the top quintiles in all the countries other than Sweden, it appears that the differences in rank are mainly due to differences in the welfare shares of the lowest quintiles.

For members of two-parent families, the ranking by the share of the bottom or the top quintiles is somewhat different from the

Table 6.9 Distribution of welfare positions of one-parent and two-parent families by quintiles of persons for five countries (except Israel)[1]

Country	Quintiles of persons				
	1	2	3	4	5
Sweden					
Two-parent families	10.93	16.58	19.53	23.00	29.96
One-parent families	11.76	16.50	20.19	22.90	28.66
West Germany					
Two-parent families	10.43	14.14	17.11	20.97	37.34
One-parent families	6.28	12.57	17.82	23.65	39.68
United Kingdom					
Two-parent families	10.43	14.98	18.68	22.68	33.23
One-parent families	9.72	12.83	16.39	22.58	38.49
Canada					
Two-parent families	8.68	14.77	18.52	23.41	34.62
One-parent families	5.88	11.19	16.07	24.99	41.86
United States					
Two-parent families	7.76	14.31	18.88	24.11	34.93
One-parent families	4.86	11.47	16.02	24.49	43.15

1. Countries implicitly ranked according to the relative welfare position of one-parent families as in Table 6.2.

ranking by Gini coefficients. While Sweden and the United Kingdom get the same rank by all measures, the ranks for the other countries differ. West Germany's rank for the bottom quintile (3) is better than its Gini rank (4), which in turn is better than its top quintile rank (5), thus indicating less inequality within the lowest welfare group and more within the highest. Canada changes its rank only in relation to the lowest group, while the United States does so only in respect of the highest group. Finally, it should be noted that differences among the shares of the bottom quintile are much smaller in the case of members of two-parent families than for those of one-parent families, thus indicating a greater diversity among countries as regards one-parent families.

If the results using this welfare measure are grouped in classes, calculated as percentages of an overall average of the welfare measure, differences in the distributions are revealed from a different angle.

Table 6.10 Distribution of persons in one-parent and two-parent families by welfare position classes for five countries (except Israel)[1]

Country Type of family Persons living in	Welfare position class as percentage of overall welfare position			
	<50%	50–100%	100–150%	>150%
Sweden				
In two-parent family	5.43	54.37	35.38	4.82
In one-parent family	10.71	67.02	20.34	(1.93)[2]
West Germany				
In two-parent family	12.50	65.53	17.89	4.08
In one-parent family	36.35	48.34	11.43	3.88
United Kingdom				
In two-parent family	22.10	50.17	22.41	5.32
In one-parent family	40.63	43.44	11.41	4.52
Canada				
In two-parent family	15.53	52.63	24.36	7.48
In one-parent family	53.25	32.20	12.12	2.43
United States				
In two-parent family	18.00	46.63	26.98	8.39
In one-parent family	60.93	28.90	8.21	1.96

1. Countries implicitly ranked according to relative welfare positions of one-parent families as in Table 6.2.
2. Derived from less than 20 households in the sample.

As can be gathered from Table 6.10, in each country far more than 50 per cent of members of both family types are below the average welfare position and the proportions of members of one-parent families are always greater (78–90 per cent) than those of two-parent families (60–78 per cent), indicating their worse relative position. Ranking countries by these proportions reproduces the Gini ranks for one-parent families but not for two-parent families. While Sweden maintains its top rank, West Germany changes to fifth and the United Kingdom to fourth.

If one-half of the overall average welfare position is taken as a 'low welfare line', the sizes of the corresponding 'low welfare groups' can be compared. This again reveals that the frequency of members of one-parent families is much greater (11–61 per cent) than that of members of two-parent families (5–22 per cent) in all countries, and that the divergences between countries regarding

Table 6.11 Distribution of persons in one-parent and two-parent families by number of children and welfare position classes for five countries (except Israel)[1]

Country	Welfare position class as percentage of overall average welfare position			
	<50%	50–100%	100–150%	>150%
Sweden				
Two-parent family/one child	$(3.6)^2$	32.5	53.8	10.1
One-parent family/one child	$(7.4)^2$	61.3	29.9	$(1.4)^2$
Two-parent family/two children	5.3	59.2	32.8	$(2.7)^2$
One-parent family/two children	$(10.9)^2$	76.6	$(12.5)^2$	$(—)^2$
Two-parent family/three and more	$(8.6)^2$	76.6	$(13.2)^2$	$(1.2)^2$
One-parent family/three and more	$(28.0)^2$	$(64.0)^2$	$(—)^2$	$(8.0)^2$
West Germany				
Two-parent family/one child	5.31	59.87	28.35	6.45
One-parent family/one child	30.70	42.09	21.05	5.85
Two-parent family/two children	13.56	71.28	11.74	3.48
One-parent family/two children	38.76	57.30	$(3.93)^2$	$(—)^2$
Two-parent family/three and more	23.23	63.39	12.37	$(1.14)^2$
One-parent family/three and more	47.37	45.62	$(—)^2$	$(7.02)^2$
United Kingdom				
Two-parent family/one child	3.77	50.32	34.60	11.32
One-parent family/one child	31.25	45.83	$(15.63)^2$	$(7.30)^2$
Two-parent family/two children	7.11	61.15	26.64	5.09
One-parent family/two children	37.36	41.76	$(10.99)^2$	$(5.49)^2$
Two-parent family/three and more	22.10	61.48	14.22	$(2.19)^2$
One-parent family/three and more	56.09	$(36.59)^2$	$(7.31)^2$	$(—)^2$
Canada				
Two-parent family/one child	14.56	34.82	55.05	22.02
One-parent family/one child	42.34	34.18	19.39	$(4.68)^2$
Two-parent family/two children	11.59	55.90	25.96	6.54
One-parent family/two children	50.39	37.98	$(9.30)^2$	$(2.32)^2$
Two-parent family/three and more	25.93	59.68	11.54	$(2.66)^2$
One-parent family/three and more	75.86	$(20.69)^2$	$(1.72)^2$	$(—)^2$

Table 6.11 Continued

Country	Welfare position class as percentage of overall average welfare position			
	<50%	50–100%	100–150%	>150%
United States				
Two-parent family/one child	10.95	35.83	36.66	16.56
One-parent family/one child	40.96	39.21	15.50	4.32
Two-parent family/two children	13.64	48.70	30.09	7.56
One-parent family/two children	57.69	32.84	7.81	1.66
Two-parent family/three and more	28.91	53.01	15.33	2.70
One-parent family/three and more	82.32	15.56	$(1.94)^2$	$(—)^2$

1. Countries implicitly ranked according to relative welfare position of one-parent families as in Table 6.2.
2. Derived from less than 20 households in the sample.

one-parent families are much larger. Ranking countries by their proportions of members of one-parent families below the 'low welfare line' results in the same ranking as in the case of relative welfare positions of one-parent families, i.e. the ranking is slightly different from that produced by using the Gini coefficient. Looking at the distribution of persons, the overall picture is thus confirmed although slight differences between the United Kingdom and West Germany are revealed in the lower part of the distribution.

At the beginning of this section, it was hypothesised that the relative positions of families decrease with an increasing number of children due to reductions in earnings capacity, and that this is even more likely to be the case for one-parent families. Table 6.11 reveals a few tendencies which support this hypothesis:

1. The proportions of members of one-parent families below the low welfare line (50 per cent of the average economic welfare position) are always higher than those for members of two-parent families.

2. The proportions of members of both family types below the 50 per cent low welfare line increase with an increase in the number of children (except in Canada for two-parent families with one or two children).
3. Family size increases generally lead to greater increases in the proportions of members of one-parent families than of two-parent families below the 50 per cent low welfare line.

The final conclusion from Table 6.11 is that the relative position of most of the one-parent families with three or more children is extremely miserable. The public transfer systems in each of the countries are obviously not able to keep all of these families at least at the 50 per cent low welfare line. This is all the more an unsolved social problem since most of the members of these families obviously are children.

SUMMARY

One-parent families are considered to be a social problem in many countries. Up to now comparative studies of the relative economic position of one-parent families were based upon hypothetical family types using average earnings or percentages thereof, and calculating social transfers according to the social security regulations of the countries under review.

This study on the one hand compares the economic position of one-parent families as indicated by their average net income per adult equivalent unit in six countries and on the other compares differences in the income distributions of one-parent and two-parent families. Differences in factor income, private transfers, public transfers, taxes and social security contributions are considered to be the main determinants of differences among countries in the relative economic positions of one-parent families. If countries are ranked by the relative economic position of their one-parent families, it is found that the first rank of Sweden is due to a high labour force participation of lone parents and generous and comprehensive public transfers. West Germany's second rank results from high labour force participation but much less generous public transfers in favour of one-parent families. Israel and the UK mainly rely upon public transfers but can only secure a middle rank position. Canada and the USA show medium labour force participation, but rather low and mainly means-tested transfers, thus reaching only low rank positions.

Considering distributional aspects, the welfare positions of one-parent families are generally less equally distributed than the positions of two-parent families. The ranking of countries by inequality measures for one-parent families is similar to that found by using the relative economic positions of these groups. By defining a 'low welfare line' it is shown that high proportions of one-parent families with more than two minor children are in a very disadvantageous position, thus constituting an unsolved social problem.

NOTES

We thank the Ford Foundation, the Government of Luxemburg, Computer Resources Inc. and the German Research Foundation (DFG) for their financial support. We also thank Günther Schmaus for the basic calculations from the LIS data files, Doris Linder for her research assistance and Irene Becker for adjusting the West German data file to the LIS conventions. Grateful acknowledgement is due for valuable comments by Anita Pfaff and Richard Hemming who discussed a preliminary version of this chapter at the LIS Conference in Luxemburg.

1. A fourth economic dimension of living conditions consists of a family's net wealth. This factor is not dealt with because of lack of wealth data in the LIS database.
2. These definitions, both for one-parent and two-parent families, fully correspond to the definitions used in the Swedish dataset. Datasets of other countries had to be recalculated.
3. In discussing the earnings capacity of a family, we have implicitly given priority to the duties of child care and treated the available work time as a residual. This is a simplification since the time necessary for child care cannot be determined objectively. The utilisation of time, however, is part of a family's decision. Hence, the time used for child care and the quality of child care ought to be a dimension for comparison, too.
4. 'Unknown' means that the name and/or address of second parent are not known for legal procedures to enforce maintenance liabilities.
5. For example if a divorcee with children remarries, the maintenance claims of the children against their natural parent usually do not cease. In this case the new two-parent family might receive private transfers.
6. This summary account is based on material in Kamerman and Kahn (1983), Shamai (1985) and others. A fuller description and comparison can be found in Hauser and Fischer (1986).

7 · THE SIGNIFICANCE OF LIS FOR COMPARATIVE SOCIAL POLICY RESEARCH

Michael O'Higgins, Lee Rainwater and Timothy M. Smeeding

INTRODUCTION

Since 1970, social scientific use of household income survey data for policy analysis both within academia and government has increased dramatically. The capacity to describe the effects of existing policy and simulate the effects of changes in policy is well established in most modern nations, especially those with elaborate welfare states. Microsimulation models in individual countries provide policy makers with increasingly detailed analytic insights into the effects of policy changes on participant behaviour (labour supply, savings), on public budgets and on family well-being (poverty status).

However, while the techniques used, for example, in Canada and West Germany are similar, the analyses are almost always limited to one country. It seems reasonable that the next step in improving policy analysis comes from moving to a cross-national focus using comparable income surveys in a number of countries. As the previous papers in this volume have suggested, this is the primary goal of LIS. That is, it constitutes a databank of household income surveys that can be used by scholars and policy analysts to study the effects of different kinds of programmes on poverty, income adequacy in retirement and the distribution of economic well-being generally.

The purpose of this chapter is to explain the significance of LIS for social policy research, not only as it currently exists, but as it may become in the future. While LIS presents the researcher with the broad new venues and opportunities of comparing several countries *within* one single paper or book, it also creates a demand for additional historical, institutional and legal knowledge about the countries which are being studied. While these demands may discourage some researchers, they are obstacles which can in most cases be more easily overcome. In fact, the enormous benefits which are likely to emerge from LIS-based research will almost certainly outweigh these costs. In the same way that household panel data have slowly revolutionised national policy research, a cross-national databank such as LIS presents new opportunities which may in turn have a lasting impact on social policy research. The rest of this chapter discusses some of these opportunities and their significance.

The following section begins by advancing the general attractiveness of cross-national analysis as a perspective from which national policy can be viewed and compared. The next two sections move the discussion more directly into policy research in general and income comparisons in particular. The concluding section discusses the future developments which are planned and foreseen in LIS and the way that these changes will further facilitate comparative social policy research.

LEARNING ABOUT SOCIETIES FROM COMPARISON

A central concern in each of the social science disciplines is to describe how modern industrial societies have changed over the past decades and to model those changes in terms of variables of central interest to each discipline. The first task is to determine what has happened; the second to test hypotheses concerning the causes of the observed changes, that is to try to explain social change.

It seems clear that modern advanced societies have common core structures: human and non-human resources, human needs and systems or institutions for linking the two. However, institutions have evolved differently because of a variety of social and political factors which together with demographic change and economic health produce the measures of income and its composition which LIS has aggregated and made comparable. The fascinating challenge which LIS presents to the social science researcher is the opportunity to try to disentangle these factors and to link causally the LIS outcome differences to economic, social, political, demographic, institutional or other changes.

In this way, one can learn about the uniqueness and/or commonness of any particular one society by comparing it with other societies. In other words, comparisons across countries provide variance in the economic, social and institutional unit of analysis which bring out features of that unit which would not otherwise be recognisable. Hence to the social scientific methodological toolkit of historical analysis by which we vary time by age group (cohort studies) or by individual situational change (panel studies), we can add another perspective: that of cross-national comparison.

The closest intra-country analogy is that of interstate or interprovincial differences in some variable which allow insights into how these differences are or are not related to interstate differences in other variables. While formal modelling is also necessary to distinguish causal relationships from those which merely represent correlations, the benefits from this mode of investigation should not be discounted. For example Bane and Ellwood (1986) presented evidence that differences in interstate rates of teenage illegitimacy in the United States are not related to differences in the generosity of welfare benefits for single-parent families (or incomes, or racial composition) across states. One could envision a similar cross-national comparison of illegitimacy *vis-à-vis* social support benefit levels for single parents.

While a study like Bane and Ellwood's has the advantage of 'holding constant' federal government and other 'national' influences on illegitimacy, it also limits the scope to only national comparisons. A similar cross-country comparison would both enrich the analysis (by going beyond federal or national policies), while at the same time making it more difficult owing to the additional variables which vary across countries, e.g. different institutions for social support for illegitimate children and their parents. Both the potential and the difficulties of comparative cross-national social science research can be thus illustrated.

A better-known example from the political and sociological perspective is the well-known effort to test various hypotheses about the development of the welfare state using data on the social and political characteristics of society as predictors of the level of welfare state effort (Wilensky, 1975; Korpi and Esping-Andersen, 1985). However, these studies reflect largely aggregative analyses with 'societies' or 'countries' or 'groups of countries' (continental, Scandinavian, etc.) as the unit of analysis. The uniqueness of LIS is its ability to go *beneath* this level, to the families or individuals *within* the country, thus creating additional variance in experiences within the comparative research framework.

But, as the papers in this volume have shown, it is not necessary to begin with full blown behavioural models to begin to analyse data comparatively. That is, comparative research can be either exploratory or descriptive or based on formal hypothesis testing. Much can be learned simply by laying out the facts of how societies are similar or different with respect to particular matters of interest. The exploratory papers in this volume have pointed out large outcome differences, e.g. in elderly poverty, which cannot be simply explained by demography, economic differences or other simplistic hypotheses. As this type of work moves from initial exploratory or descriptive efforts to formal hypothesis testing, the analyst is pushed to tinker further with the new opportunities of comparative social science. Just how much can be learned about one society by comparing its people to those in another society will be the legacy of LIS.

COMPARATIVE POLICY INSIGHTS

Because advanced industrial societies have many common goals and common problems it is possible to look at the political systems of different countries as a range of experiments for solving common problems. In this way, one can investigate how well the solutions that different countries adopt to these common problems work. In order to do this it is necessary to establish the extent to which the goals for policy are different or similar from country to country and then to investigate how those goals interact with the different socio-economic circumstances of the countries to produce the outcomes which LIS presents. Certain problems, e.g. access to health care, income deprivation and poverty, low wages, old age and unemployment, are sufficiently general to provide a good starting place for traditional social science research issues such as those which are explored in this volume.

Yet other areas of public policy analysis could benefit from comparative research, though to date, little such analysis can be found in most large country daily news sources, particularly in the United States. For instance, take the case of product recall for defective craftmanship.

The US media is replete with stories of a particular international automobile model which is being recalled owing to sudden unexpected acceleration problems. However, in none of these stories has there been any discussion of the fact that this automobile is sold in a number of different countries. It would be interesting to know first of all whether the problem exists in all countries or whether it is only Americans who are able to get automobiles which accelerate in this way. If the problem does exist in other countries, then it would be very interesting to study how the problem is dealt with in those countries both by government and by the corporation. Do different political and legal structures imply different legal product liability situations, and hence different responses by government, by corporations, and/or by both?

Similar opportunities exist in other realms of public policy. A few examples include public health policy and AIDS; immigration and differential fertility leading to 'minority' population expansion as compared to majority population 'baby bust' population shrinkage; and public policy measures related to nuclear accidents.

As alluded to earlier, policy studies confined to a single country tend to be highly parochial because they take as given things which vary across countries. That is, they take as given matters that are in fact social and political choices. The value of a comparative focus is that it forces the analyst to look at how choices are made and issues are selected in different countries where policy itself is a variable. Precisely because countries differ in such factors as industrial structure, economic openness, welfare state regimes, and family and labour market policies, comparative datasets like LIS offer the chance to study such phenomena. These factors cannot be found with cross-section or even panel data from any given country because there is little or no variation in these institutions and factors within countries over even a 20 year period. To assess the impact of such factors on variations in social and economic well-being, a cross-national dataset is required. Without such a cross-national perspective, scientific and policy analyses tend to take as given important policy variables; in other words, these variables are treated as constants.

Several large countries are just beginning to consider these comparative policy analysis opportunities. For instance, the high value of comparative international social policy research in the United States and the United Kingdom has only most recently been stressed by a joint report by the US National Science Foundation and the UK Economic and Social Research Council (Jowell *et al.*, 1985), by the National Academy of Sciences and the National Institute of Aging in the USA, and by several distinguished researchers at recent US Congressional hearings on future directions for social science research. In order to provide a firm foundation for such research, comparable social science databases must rank as a high priority item (Jowell *et al.*, 1985). Without comparable data true international comparative policy research is difficult at best, and often impossible (e.g. the uproar following the OECD report on comparative income distributions by Sawyer, 1976). It is precisely this void into which LIS began to throw itself. As LIS grows and matures, it will provide the wherewithal to perform increasingly sophisticated analyses of social policy (e.g. microsimulation analyses) across a wider range of countries and over a longer time horizon.

COMPARATIVE INCOME ANALYSIS

The papers in this volume begin to demonstrate the usefulness of LIS in comparative analyses of income and its composition. In the future LIS should continue to be extremely useful in both basic and applied income research concerned with issues such as the following:

1. The distribution of household income and the relative income positions of the old and the young; urban and rural residents, and other groups of policy interest, e.g. single parents and elderly widows.
2. The distribution of earnings for both men and women, the contribution of wives' earnings to family income, and their change over the worker's life cycle, including the transition to retirement.
3. Comparative studies of the workings of the welfare state and its income transfer policies towards the elderly, the disabled and the unemployed.
4. The importance of private pension and property income in supplanting social insurance income among the elderly to achieve reasonable pre-retirement earning replacement rates for the retired elderly.
5. The effectiveness of universalist child benefits, unemployment insurance and means-tested benefits in preventing poverty among children.

As this volume indicates, the LIS database has already been used to study income poverty, the relative economic status of one-parent families and of the elderly, and the overall distribution of income and of government cash transfers and direct taxes.

LIS DEVELOPMENTS AND POLICY RESEARCH

Despite the youth of LIS, already a number of improvements and modifications in LIS have begun to be achieved. Here only four of them are discussed:

1. The addition of non-cash income.
2. The development of a historical database by updating and backdating LIS.
3. The addition of labour force survey data to complement income surveys.
4. The merging of income microdata with macro-economic, demographic and programme data to provide an easily manageable aggregative database which is more flexible and relevant to both policy and policy analysis than the usual social indicators/public expenditure volumes published by such groups as the ILO or the United Nations.

Non-cash income

Almost from the initiation of LIS, the proponents were acutely aware of the limitations of cash income as a measure of economic well-being. From a purely methodological perspective, ignoring in-kind transfers can distort both comparisons of economic inequality between countries and measures of relative income within countries as Smeeding (1985) has recently demonstrated by comparing cash and non-cash incomes for the US elderly with the rest of the US population.

While non-cash income benefits both the elderly (especially via non-cash medical, food and housing transfers) and the non-elderly (especially via fringe benefits), the former group realises a net gain of between 5 and 9 percentage points in terms of the relative income ratio of elderly to non-elderly once non-cash incomes are taken into account. Moreover, the inclusion of non-cash income reduces measures of income inequality among the elderly by a much larger proportion than it reduces inequality among the US non-elderly. Excluding major food, housing and medical benefits in measuring economic well-being for the elderly in the United States during 1979 is tantamount to excluding 28 per cent of their aggregate after-tax income (Smeeding, 1985).

Further, the relative importance of non-cash and cash transfers differs from country to country, as does the relative importance of particular types of non-cash transfers (e.g. see OECD, 1985). Furthermore, particular forms of non-cash transfer may be valued differently by recipients (and/or by donors) both within and between countries. These differences are important to any debate on policy alternatives, for the prospects of special provision for a given good, and to the methodological issues surrounding the measurement of the distribution of economic well-being.

Policy questions related to non-cash income have assumed major importance in a range of countries. For instance, in a recent article Aaron (1984) asks how much reliance should be placed on in-kind versus cash assistance in the United States. Recent public sector expenditure trends have emphasised growth in the former either through direct subsidy or through indirect (tax expenditure) subsidy. However, government deficits and the rapidly rising costs of major non-cash benefit programmes, particularly in the health care area (Meyer, 1984), have led to

new efforts to reduce these outlays and/or to shift their finance
to other sources (employers, families or the private non-profit
sector). At the same time, expected demographic changes will
add further pressures to increase outlays.

How will countries cope with this problem: via higher taxes,
reduced benefits or greater reliance on other types or forms of
payments (e.g. families, employers or charities)? The lessons
learned from the experience of various modern welfare state
countries in dealing with this problem alone may yield significant
new policy ideas for the United States where, among other
pressing problems, the Medicare programme is in serious financial
straits (e.g. see Aiken and Bays, 1984), or for West Germany
where old age health and cash benefits are nearly 20 per cent of
GDP. Data on the mixture, receipt and financing of various non-
cash income components in modern countries will help facilitate
these comparisons in a meaningful way.

Similarly, the effect of in-kind transfers on poverty in the
United States has been well established. Once major food,
medical and housing transfers are included, between 12 and 45
per cent of those poor before transfer are lifted over the official
US poverty line (Smeeding, 1982) depending on how these
benefits are valued. International poverty measurement is affected
in much the same way. The current LIS database indicates a
poverty rate of 5.0 per cent for Sweden in 1979 if account is
taken of both cash and near-cash benefits (see Chapter 3). If
rental housing rebates are not counted, however, the Swedish
poverty rate increases to 9.0 per cent. Including these benefits
gives Sweden the second lowest poverty rate among the seven
LIS countries; excluding them, the Swedes drop to only the fourth
lowest poverty rate. The effect of other truly 'non-cash' benefits
on poverty has not been counted in any LIS country other than
the United States. It seems likely that counting these benefits in
addition to those near-cash items now readily available will affect
both the absolute and relative levels of poverty within and among
LIS countries. Work is currently underway to allow the effects
of such adjustments to be available in the LIS database.

Historical LIS database

As mentioned earlier in this chapter, a major role of the social
sciences is to describe how modern advanced societies have

changed over recent decades, particularly with respect to developing policies designed to meet major emerging social needs: growing numbers of retired elderly, high unemployment, single-parent families, etc. The need to model these changes cuts across all of the social science disciplines: sociology (role of family); demography (baby boom and bust); economics (employment, growth, inflation), and all are relevant to public policy. With an adequate database one can both determine what happened (e.g. how incomes change, how family size and composition change) and then test hypotheses concerning why these changes took place (because of economic factors, demographic factors, policy-induced behavioural change, etc.). But the database must be long term in order to capture subtle but substantive changes in social and political institutions as well as short-term economic swings.

The creation of a multi-year, multi-nation LIS databank will facilitate such concerns for several reasons. First, the description of social change clearly is dependent on data at several points in time, and a series of cross-sectional surveys will serve this purpose well. Second, in the attempt to explain social change, a focus on cohorts, or specifically on individual change over the life course, becomes central. A series of cross-sectional surveys may not be the ideal type of data to study individual changes over the life course, but it is superior to a single cross-sectional survey, because it allows the researcher to follow birth cohorts of individuals over time. We cannot trace an individual's life course but we can describe well the collective experience of a birth cohort during segments of the life course.

Because of the enormous complexity of institutionalised labour markets and social programmes and policies, there is a tendency for policy debate and policy making in these areas to proceed on the basis of many different false impressions and untested assumptions. It is likely that over the next decade there will be a pressing need for systematic analysis of nations' experience over the past several decades with these kinds of programmes and policies. The databank to be assembled at LIS should be an extremely valuable tool for policy analysis of the many different questions which arise now and in the future concerning societal choices about claims on economic resources.

Labour force data

Perhaps the largest gap in LIS as it currently stands is the lack of adequate labour force participation and level of employment data. Because most country databases underlying LIS concentrate on family income and its sources, and not on the supply and demand for employment, LIS is not at present well suited to carry out linkages between changes in work and its relationship to the welfare state. As intermittent and long-term unemployment continues to be a major social problem, as labour force participation of women continues to grow in importance, and as early retirement ceases to be unusual in Western societies, the need for LIS databases to capture not only income composition but also labour force participation increases.

To the extent that additional information on not only labour force attachment but also on wages and marginal tax rates (both the tax rates resulting from employment-related income and payroll taxes, and those arising from transfer programme benefit reduction rates) can be added to the existing rich LIS data on income transfers, the potential for LIS to be used in behavioural microsimulation models wil be enhanced. Concerns with topics such as labour supply response to public income transfer programme changes, tax avoidance behaviour via the hidden economy and the impact of transfer programmes on private savings rates can be studied using these parameters.

In general, most key relationships between market income (in particular earnings) and social transfer income hinge on being able to observe and model movements between these income sources, whether related to schooling, unemployment, retirement or disability. As the LIS project moves forwards to update the 1979 and 1981 files to the mid-1980s, this will be one of the principal concerns and priorities.

Micro–macro linkage

A further development would be to expand the LIS database by linking it to material on economic, demographic and public programme changes in the countries. It is increasingly common for single country macroeconomic databases to be accessible on-line, and the relevant major international organisations such as the OECD and the International Monetary Fund have multi-country databases. The same is true of demographic data.

A link between the LIS database and such datafiles would be helpful to researchers doing cross-country studies at one point in time by providing immediate access to material on the different points on the demographic and economic performance cycles at which each country was to be found at the relevant point in time. But for multi-year research the value of such links would be geometrically greater. Not only would the additional data facilitate the researcher's understanding in a descriptive way, but such access would greatly increase the possibility of modelling the relationships between changes across time in the income variables and in the demographic and macro-economic variables.

The obvious extension of this would be to build in to the database descriptions of the salient features of social programmes and public provision in the different countries. Even the most experienced cross-national researcher readily admits (or is rapidly made aware of) the limits of her or his detailed knowledge of social programmes in more than two or three countries. Even when descriptive material in paper form is at hand at the LIS headquarters, the search time can be considerable and the layout of information often does little to assist comparisons. Furthermore, such availability will not greatly assist those working from a remote site by telecommunication linkage to the LIS database.

A linked database, which identified social provisions in a way that was related to the income and other variable classifications in LIS, would greatly assist understanding of the institutional reasons for outcome differences between countries and across time. With the development of expert systems, it might then become possible to use such information in model-based analyses of public policy, and thus move further beyond descriptive and intuitive explanation.

These projected developments open up a further possibility in the medium-term – that of creating the basis for a cross-national simulation model which can draw on real country data. If one started with a common demographic database, the enriched LIS data would then allow national parameters for the proportion of the population in different demographic categories, with different levels and patterns of earnings and transfers, etc., to be introduced and varied as is already done in simulations of interprovince or interstate differences. Such models cannot properly be constructed without access to microdata which capture the complexity of patterns of income access and family structure at the unit level: the enriched LIS database will provide such access to comparable data across a wide range of industrialised countries.

CONCLUSIONS

This chapter has discussed some of what has emerged from the LIS project, and some of the plans and possibilities for the future. The progress thus far has been both interesting and encouraging for those involved, and the prospects are exciting. But two more general points deserve emphasis in closing this first LIS book.

Despite its unique and novel nature, LIS is essentially nothing more than a common-sense adaptation of research methods to the additional possibilities made available by the advances in information systems and the greater availability of microdata within individual countries. LIS would hardly have been possible ten years ago; in ten years' time, we venture to suggest, its principles – and, we hope, its practice – will be commonplace. Just as social research within countries has increasingly come to be based on analyses of microdata rather than of manipulations of published grouped data, so too international comparisons will need to use the richness of microdata in order to profit more thoroughly from the complex insights of comparative social research.

Second, this book has primarily presented the results of the first sets of analyses carried out by those initially involved in the construction of the LIS database – but LIS was created as a database for the social research and policy analysis community as a whole. The Appendix to this book describes the variables available in the first wave of LIS and indicates how further information and access can be obtained. The eventual measure of the success of LIS will be the regular use of the database by this wider community.

NOTE

The authors are grateful for the support of the Ford Foundation, the US National Science Foundation and the Government of Luxemburg through the Centre for Population, Poverty and Policy Studies (CEPS). They have benefited from the suggestions and insights of all those involved in the LIS project, but the opinions presented here are theirs alone.

APPENDIX: A USER'S GUIDE TO THE LIS DATABASE

INTRODUCTION

With funding initially provided by the Ford Foundation and subsequently by an international consortium of science foundations, research councils and centres, and government agencies in member countries, LIS has now moved beyond the initial experimental stage to provide a databank which can be updated and expanded to include the most recent data available for nations with high quality income microdata sets which choose to participate. By the beginning of 1989, the dataset had been expanded to cover ten countries – Australia, Canada, West Germany, Israel, the Netherlands, Norway, Sweden, Switzerland, the United Kingdom and the United States. It is anticipated that datasets from Austria, Denmark, Finland, France, Ireland, Luxemburg, Italy and Poland will be added to LIS by 1990. A further expansion to include Belgium, Greece, New Zealand, Spain, Japan, Hungary and other countries is at the planning stage. In addition, the existing LIS dataset will be updated during 1989 at which time datasets for 1985 or 1986 will be added for almost all current LIS countries.

By the beginning of 1989, the LIS project contained ten consistent microdata sets. In addition to the seven sets described in Table 1.1, the database included the Australian Income and Housing Survey, 1981–82 (sample size: 17,000; sampling frame: population census), the Dutch Survey of Income and Programme Users (1983), sample size: 4,800; sampling frame: address register of the post and telephone companies), and the Swiss Income and Wealth Survey 1982 (sample size: 7,000; sampling frame: electoral register and central register of resident foreigners). All datasets contain detailed information on income (by source), taxes, and household or family composition. Tables A.1 and A.2 summarily list the income and sociodemographic variables currently available for each LIS country.

172

Accessing the LIS database

The LIS project and dataset is permanently housed at the CEPS Research Centre in Luxemburg. Privacy and confidentiality promises to LIS country statistical agencies prohibit public use datafiles for general distribution. All prospective users must specify the nature of their projected research and sign a pledge not to violate the privacy and confidentiality of country datasets and the survey respondents. The LIS data are stored on the Government of Luxemburg's computers and can be accessed only via several CRTs at the CEPS Centre. A new and sophisticated data packing and on-line tabulation package, CRISP, has been developed in conjunction with the LIS project by Computer Resources International (CRI). This program can be used to process quickly and efficiently either remote or on-site data requests through the Centre and to monitor output transmission.

Those wishing to use the dataset can follow one of three logistical approaches:

1. Researchers connected to the EARN/BITNET network in the United States or in Europe can send properly formatted data requests directly to Luxemburg where the technical staff will review and process the request. Once the data have been processed and checked, output can then be sent back to the user using the same network. This allows easy access at reasonable speed (1–2 days) and low cost. The user package (see below) gives the prospective user all the necessary information and job control language to submit a remote request. The EARN/BITNET system allows the easiest and most cost-effective approach to use the LIS database. (EARN/BITNET is an international inter-university telecommunications network. Any university with an IBM or VAX mainframe computer can become a BITNET node. The mainframe stores messages and output until the receiver retrieves them. The CEPS–LIS project centre is one of these nodes, as are most major European and US universities.)

2. The researcher can post data requests (in disk form) and receive the data output by mail. While the money cost of this method is only slightly more than that of using EARN/BITNET, the time frame increases to two weeks at a minimum. However, this does provide access to those researchers who are not connected to EARN/BITNET but who wish to use the database.

3. The researcher can make plans to spend some time at the CEPS Centre working with the LIS staff and preparing SPSSX data requests under their supervision. Living quarters at low cost rates can be arranged in this case.

The requirement that data requests be written by the user reduces communication errors and data processing costs, both in terms of time

Table A.1 LIS income variable summary matrix[1]

Variable	United States	United Kingdom	Norway	Canada	West Germany	Israel	Sweden	Switzerland	Australia	Netherlands
V1 Wage and salary income	X	X	X	X	X	X	X	X	X	X
V2 Mandatory employer contributions	X		X		X	X	X	X	None	X
V3 Nonmandatory employer contributions	X							X	None	in V2
V4 Farm self-employment income	X	X	X	X	X	No farm	X	X	X	in V5
V5 Nonfarm self-employment income	X	X	X	X	X	X	X	X	X	X
V6 In kind earnings		X	X				Some in V1			
V7 Mandatory contributions for self-employed	X	X	X		X	X	X	X	None	see V2 & V13
V8 Cash property income	X	X	X	X	X	X	X	X	X	X
V9 Noncash property income	X	X	X		X	X	X	(X)		X
V10 Home value	X	X	X	X	X	X	X	in V8		X
V11 Income tax	X	X	X		X	X	X	X	X	X
V12 Property or wealth tax	X	X	X		X	X	X	X		X
V13 Mandatory employee contributions	X	X	X		X	X	None	X	None	X
V14 Other direct taxes					X		None	None	None	
V15 Indirect taxes					X				NA	
V16 Sick pay	in V1	in V17	in V1	in V36	in V1	in V1	X	in V1	None	in V1
V17 Accident pay	X	X	X	in V24	X		in V16	in V1	X	in V1
V18 Disability pay	X	X	in V17	in V19 & V21	V17	X	in V16 & V19	X	X	X
V19 Social retirement	X	X	in V17	X	X	X	X	X	X	X
V20 Child allowance	None	X	X	X	X	X	X	in V1	X	X
V21 Unemployment pay	X	X	In V17 or NA?	X	X	X	X	X	X	X

V22 Maternity allowance	None	X	in V17	in V19 & V24	in V1	X	X	None	in V1	X	None	None or in V1
V23 Military, veterans or war related benefits	in V18	in V18	in V17	X	X	X	None	X	X	X	X	X
V24 Other social insurance	X	X	in V17	X	X	X	X	X	X	X	X	X
V25 Cash benefits	X	X	X	X	X	X	X	X	X	X	X	X
V26 Near cash benefits	X	X	X	in V25	in V25	X	X	X	X	X		
V27 Food benefits	X	X										
V28 Housing benefits	X	X										
V29 Medical benefits	X	X										X
V30 Heating allowance	in V25	X										
V31 Education benefits	X	X								X	X	X
V32 Private pensions	X	X	X	X	X	in V32	in V19	X	X	X	X	in V32
V33 Public sector pensions	X	X	X	in V36	in V32	in V32	in V19	X	X	in V32	in V32	in V32
V34 Alimony/child support	X, some in V35	X	X	in V36	X	X	X	X	X	X	X	X
V35 Other regular	X, some in V34	X	X	in V36	X	X	X	in V34	in V34	in V34	None	None
V36 Other cash income	X	X	X	X	X	X	X	X	X	X	X	X
V37 Realised lump sum income	X	X	X	X			X					
V38 Total (or net) income question	X	X	X		X	X	X	X	X	X	X	X
V39 Head's pay	X	X	X	X	X	X	X	X	X	X	X	X
V40 Head's wage	X	X	X	X	X	X	X	X	X	X	X	X
V41 Spouse's pay	X	X	X	X	X	X	X	X	X	X	X	X
V42 Spouse's wage	X	X	X	X	X	X	X	X	X	X	X	X

Table is coded as follows:
X: separately recorded source.
None: no such income source.
blank: not available on dataset.
Combined variables are indicated as well.

Table A.2 LIS demographic summary matrix

Variable	United States	United Kingdom	Norway	Canada	West Germany	Israel	Sweden	Switzerland	Australia	Netherlands
D1 Age head	X	X	X	X	X	X	X	X	X	X
D2 Age spouse	X	X	X	X	X	X	X	X	X	X
D3 Sex head	X	X	X	X	X	X	X	X	X	X
D4 Number persons	X	X	X	X	X	X	X	X	X	X
D5 Relatedness	X	X	X	X	X	X	X	X	X	X
D6 Number earners	X	X	X	X	X	X	X	X	X	X
D7 Non-farm – farm	X		X	X	X		X	X	X	
D8 Ethnicity head	X				X	X		X		
D9 Race head	X									
D10 Education head	X		X	X		X	X	X	X	X
D11 Education spouse	X			X	X	X			X	X
D12 Occupation training head				X	X				X	X
D13 Occupation training spouse					X	X	X		X	X
D14 Occupation head	X	X	X	X		X	X	X	X	X
D15 Occupation spouse	X	X	X	X		X	X		X	X
D16 Industry head	X	X	X			X	X		X	
D17 Industry spouse	X	X	X			X	X		X	

D18	Type worker head	X	X	X	X	X		X	X	X
D19	Type worker spouse	X	X	X	X	X		X	X	X
D20	Location (urban, rural)	X	X	X	X	X	X	X	X	X
D21	Marital status head	X	X	X	X	X	X	X	X	X
D22	Tenure: owned-rented housing	X	X	X	X	X	X	X	X	X
D23	Head: full-time	X	X	X	X	X	X	X	X	X
	part-time									
D24	Spouse: full-time	X	X	X	X	X	X	X	X	X
	part-time									
D25	Disability head	X	X	X	X	X	X		X	X
D26	Disability spouse	X	X	X	X	X	in D25		X	X
D27	Number of children under 18	X	X	X	X	X	X	X	X	X
D28	Age youngest child	X	X	X	X	X	X	X	X	X
D29	Poverty status	X		X	X	X			X	X
D30	Poverty income cutoff	X		X	X	X		X	X	X

Table is coded as follows:
X: separately recorded source.

and money. The researcher is further required to make the results of research papers or reports prepared from LIS available as a LIS–CEPS Working Paper. In this way previous LIS research can be documented for those interested in furthering the use of the network.

Cost: membership and user fees

Membership in LIS is open to all countries (and national research agencies who sponsor them) and international research groups. For countries or organisations which donate country datasets to LIS, membership is open at no charge for one year. After this period, an annual membership fee will be levied. It is expected that country researchers will use the free year to find support for LIS membership in following years.

User fees are structured so as to differentiate between member country and non-member country users, and between core and project use.

The primary purpose of core funds (which are derived solely from member country fees) is to maintain and upgrade the basic datasets and the telecommunications network which facilitates access to LIS. Researchers from member countries (or member research organisations) have open and unlimited access (subject to the research confidentiality rules) to the LIS database via EARN/BITNET as a return on the core funding. In addition, member users who need LIS staff time to access the dataset are allowed up to ten days of staff time (per member country per year). At the time of writing member countries and organisations include all the countries currently in the database (except Switzerland), France (through CERC) and Luxemburg.

Researchers from non-member countries or organisations, or researchers from member countries who require extensive staff assistance (in excess of the ten day limit per year), will be charged according to the costs of staff time and related costs incurred. In effect, these users will be charged on a project use basis. The exact charges for this type of use will be determined and assessed by senior project staff, once the research request form has been completed.

Researchers (from both member and non-member countries) who are expected to make a significant contribution to LIS and related scholarly endeavours but who have low ability to meet user costs, can petition the development initiatives fund for support. A limited amount of funding to cover user fees, travel and related costs has been provided to LIS by the Ford Foundation for these purposes (see below). Interested potential users can request information on the Ford Foundation Development Initiatives Fund.

In summary, those wishing to use the LIS dataset must initially submit to either the project director or the technical director (whose addresses are listed at the end of the Appendix) a LIS Researcher Request form (which indicates the nature and scope of the analyses which the proposed research project will require) and a pledge of non-invasion of privacy.

As soon as the proposal has been reviewed, the prospective researchers will be given an estimate of the user cost (which may be zero if the researcher is from a member country and is using remote access) along with additional instructions for dataset access, if required. Cost estimates can also be provided for those who wish to prepare a large research proposal for subsequent funding.

User package

Prospective LIS users should also request the LIS user package. The user package includes a microcomputer disk with the following information: .

1. *Introduction to LIS*: a regularly updated version of introductory information.

2. *Dataset information*:

    (a) *A definition of variables list* which explains in detail the exact income components from the raw country datafile which went into each LIS variable. For demographic variables, this includes the exact wording and codes for such variables as occupation education, marital status, etc. for each country.

    (b) *Technical description* of each country datafile which goes into LIS, including sampling frame, expected sampling and non-sampling errors, reliability of income data, and other pertinent information.

    (c) *Data parameters*. For LIS income variables the maximum and minimum values, mean, median, and percentage of population receiving each type of income are included.

3. *An institutional information codebook* which includes a basic description of the social transfer programmes which provide income: history, overall outlays, eligibility rules and bibliographical sources for additional information on each such income source in each country.

4. *A list of standard recodes* of LIS income definitions (e.g. gross income, net income) and other recodes (e.g. marital status, one-parent families) for those who wish to compare their results to earlier LIS analyses using these same concepts.

5. *A sample datafile* containing a random sample of about 200 records from each country. This sample allows users to test data runs to ensure computer software commands and specifications are correct before the job is sent to Luxemburg to be run on the full database.

6. A package of *technical request information*, including available software packages and EARN/BITNET technical conventions for sending requests.

The cost of this user package, which includes all the information listed above on five standard IBM PC diskettes, is 20 US dollars or 800 Belgian francs.

RESEARCH AND TEACHING ACTIVITIES

Besides the LIS database, LIS and its parent, CEPS, sponsor several research seminars and meetings and an annual Summer Workshop Series.

LIS summer workshop series

This is a two-week pre- and post-doctoral workshop held in Luxemburg and is designed to introduce young scholars to comparative research in social policy using the LIS database. The first, very successful, workshop took place in July 1988, and subsequent workshops will be held each summer thereafter. The tuition cost includes tuition, local travel and partial board, but not international transportation. Students are expected to be subsidised by home countries, national and international research foundations, universities and other sources, including the Ford Foundation Development Initiatives Fund (see below). The language of instruction is English.

Ford Foundation Development Initiatives Fund

Under the auspices of the Ford Foundation, LIS has been granted a limited amount of funding to cover user fees, travel and related costs for scholars with a serious commitment to research in areas of the following:

1. Race, ethnicity and income disadvantage.
2. Comparisons of Eastern Europe or Latin American social welfare regimes to Western welfare state societies.

Proposals are judged on the basis of quality of proposal, relatedness to the research questions specified above and financial need. The fund can be used for scholarly research activities or to finance attendance at the summer workshop series.

LIS rules of organisation, structure and governance

LIS is a researcher-run project sponsored by a consortium of member countries, their statistical offices and social science research organisations. The administrative hierarchy and the rules of organisation and governance of LIS are available to those requesting them.

LIS newsletter

This is published twice a year. Its purpose is to publicise LIS and its services to potential users, and to communicate news about recent and planned LIS research projects, conferences and meetings. The newsletter will also include summary announcements of changes in LIS databases, new country datasets and other technical material. The newsletter is mailed free on request.

Further information on any of these aspects of LIS, and copies of the research request form, privacy pledge and the user package are available from:

LIS Technical Director
LIS-CEPS
BP65
L-7201 Walferdange
Luxemburg
(EARN/BITNET address: SSLISBB @ LUXCEP11
                       EPLISJR @ LUXCEP11)

and

Professor Timothy Smeeding
LIS Project Director
VIPPS, Vanderbilt University
1208 18th Avenue South
Nashville, Tennessee 37212
USA
(EARN/BITNET: SMEEDITM @ VUCTRVAX)

BIBLIOGRAPHY

Aaron, H. (1984) 'Six welfare questions still searching for answers', *Brookings Review*, Fall, 12–17.

Aberg, R., J. Selen and H. Tham (1985) 'Economic resources', in R. Erikson and R. Aberg (eds), *Welfare in Transition*, Oxford, Clarendon Press.

Aiken, L. and K. Bays (1984) 'The Medicare debate – round one', *New England Journal of Medicine*, November 1, 1196–200.

Allison, P.D. (1978) 'Measures of inequality', *American Sociological Review*, **43**, 865–79.

Atkinson, A. (1983) *The Economics of Inequality* (2nd edition), Oxford, Clarendon Press.

Atkinson, A. (1985) 'On the measurement of poverty', mimeo, London School of Economics (February).

Atkinson A. and J. Micklewright (1982) 'On the reliability of income data in the family expenditure survey 1970–1977', Working Paper No. 40, SSRC Programme in Taxation, Incentives and Distribution, London School of Economics (July).

Atkinson, A.B. and H. Sutherland (eds) (1988) *Tax–Benefit Models*, ST/ICERD Occasional Paper, LSE.

Bane, M.J. and D. Ellwood (1986) 'Slipping into and out of poverty: the dynamics of spells', *Journal of Human Resources*, September 1–23.

Beckerman, W. (1979) *Poverty and the Impact of Maintenance Programmes in Four Developed Countries*, Geneva, International Labour Organisation.

Cowell, F.A. (1977) *Measuring Inequality*, Oxford, Philip Allan.

Danziger, S. and M. Taussig (1977) *Conference on the Trend in Economic Inequality in the United States*, Special Report No. 11, Institute for Research on Poverty, University of Wisconsin, Madison.

Danziger, S. and M. Taussig (1979) 'The income unit and the anatomy of income distribution', *Review of Income and Wealth*, **25**(4), 365–75.

Danziger, S., J. Van der Gaag, E. Smolensky and M. Taussig (1982) 'Income transfers and the economic status of the elderly', Discussion Paper No. 695–82, Institute for Research on Poverty, University of Wisconsin, Madison.

182

European Community (1981) *Final Report from the Commission to the Council on the First Programme of Pilot Schemes and Studies to Combat Poverty*, Brussels.

Fiegehen, G. and P. Lansley (1975) 'Household size and income unit in the measurement of poverty', presented to the 14th General Conference of the IARIW, Aulanko, Finland, August.

Finer, M. (1975) *Report of the Committee on One-parent Families* (The Finer Report), London, HMSO, Cmnd 5629.

Frijs, H., L. Lauritsen and S. Scheuer (1982) *Die Familien mit nur einem Elternteil und die Armut in der EG*, Report to the Commission of the European Community, Brussels. (Document V1/2541/82 and V/2541/82).

Hauser, R. and I. Fischer (1986). 'The relative economic status of one-parent families in six major industrialised countries', SB3 Discussion Paper No. 187, University of Frankfurt, West Germany.

Hauser, R. and U. Nouvertne (1980) 'Poverty in rich countries', SB3 Discussion Paper No. 39, University of Frankfurt, West Germany.

Johannson, S. (1973) 'The level of living survey', *Acta Sociologica* **16**(3).

Jowell, R., O. Larsen and S. Reeve (1985) 'Large scale data resources for the social sciences: report of the British American Committee', prepared at the request of the UK ESRC and the US NSF, London, June.

Kahn, A.J. and S.B. Kamerman (1983) *Income Transfers for Families with Children. An Eight Country Study*, Philadelphia, Temple University Press.

Kamerman, S.B. and A.J. Kahn (eds) (1983) *Essays on Income Transfers and Related Programmes in Eight Countries*, New York, Columbia University.

Kemsley, W. *et al.* (1980) *Family Expenditure Survey Handbook*, London, HMSO.

Korpi, W (1980) 'Approaches to the study of poverty in the United States', Vincent T. Corello (ed.), *Poverty and Public Policy*, London, Oxford University Press.

Korpi W. and G. Esping-Andersen (1985) 'From poor relief to institutional welfare states', R. Eriksson (ed.), *The Scandinavian Model*, New York, M.E. Sharpe.

Kreps, J. (1976) 'The economy and the aged', in R. Binstock and E. Shanas (eds), *Handbook of Aging and the Social Sciences*, New York, Van Nostrand Reinhold.

Lazear, E. and R. Michael (1984) 'Estimating the personal distribution of income with adjustments for within-family variation', presented to Conference on the Family and the Distribution of Economic Rewards, Snowbird, Utah (September).

Max Planck Institut (1983) *Unterhaltsrecht in Europa*, Tubingen, Max Planck Institut.

Meyer, J. (1984) *The Implications of Aging Populations for Health Care Policy and Expenditure*, Paris, OECD.

Millar, J. (1985) *Lone Parents, Income Support and Living Standards: A Review of the Comparative Literature*, University of York, Social Policy Research Unit, Discussion Paper.

OECD (1976) *Public Expenditures on Income Maintenance Programmes*, Paris, OECD.

OECD (1985) *Social Expenditure: Problems of Growth and Control*, Paris, OECD.

O'Higgins, M. (1980) 'The distributive effects of public expenditure and taxation: an agnostic view of the CSO analyses', in C.T. Sandford *et al*. (eds) *Taxation and Social Policy*, London, Heinemann 29–46.

O'Higgins, M. (1985a) 'Inequality, redistribution and recession: the British experience, 1976–1982', *Journal of Social Policy* **14**(3), 297–307.

O'Higgins, M. (1985b) 'Welfare, redistribution and inequality: disillusion, illusion and reality', in P. Bean, J. Ferris and D. Whynes (eds), *In Defence of Welfare*, London, Tavistock.

O'Higgins, M. and P. Ruggles (1981) 'The distribution of public expenditures and taxes among households in the United Kingdom', *Review of Income and Wealth*, **27**(3), 298–326.

Orshansky, M. (1965) 'Counting the poor: another look at the poverty profile', *Social Security Bulletin*, **28**, 3–29.

Plotnick, R. (1984) 'A comparison of measures of horizontal inequity using alternative measures of well-being', Discussion Paper 752–84, Institute for Research on Poverty, Madison, Wisconsin.

Radner, D. (1983) 'Adjusted estimates of the size distribution of family money income', *Journal of Business and Economic Statistics* **1**(2) (April), 135–46.

Radner, D. (1985) 'Family income, age, and size of unit: selected international comparisons', *Review of Income and Wealth*, **31**(2).

Rainwater, L. (1974) *What Money Buys*, New York, Basic Books.

Rainwater, L., M. Rein and J. Schwartz (1985) *Income Packaging in the Welfare State*, Oxford, Oxford University Press.

Ramprakash, D. (1975), 'Distribution of income statistics for the United Kingdom 1972–73: sources and methods', *Economic Trends*, August.

Rein, M. (1983) 'Claims, claiming, and claims structures', in M. Rein, *From Policy to Practice*, London, Macmillan.

Riley, M. (1986) 'Overview and highlights of a sociological perspective' in A.B. Sørensen, F. Weinert and L.R. Sherrod (eds), *Human Development and the Life Course*, New Jersey, Erlbaum, 153–76.

Ringen, S. (1982). *Inntekt og forbruk i Norge, 1950–1980*, Oslo, Ministry of Consumer Affairs.

Ringen S. (1986) *Difference and Similarity: Two Studies in Comparative Income Distribution*, Stockholm, Institute for Social Research.

Rowntree, S. (1901) *Poverty – A Study of Town Life*, London, Macmillan.

Ruggles, N. and R. Ruggles (1977) 'The anatomy of earnings behaviour' in F.T. Juster (ed.), *The Distribution of Economic Well-Being*, Cambridge, Mass., Ballinger, 115–58.

Ruggles, P. and M. O'Higgins (1981) 'The distribution of public expenditure among households in the United States', *Review of Income and Wealth*, 27(2).

Ryder, N.B. (1965) 'The Cohort in the study of social change', *American Sociological Review*, 30, 843–61.

Sawyer, M. (1976) *Income Distribution in OECD Countries*, Paris, OECD.

Schwartz, J. and C. Winship (1980) 'The welfare approach to measuring inequality', in K.F. Schuessler (ed.), *Sociological Methodology*.

Shamai, N. (1985) *Child Support and One-parent Families in Israel*, National Insurance Institute Israel, Discussion Paper, April.

Smeeding, T. (1982) *Alternative Methods for Valuing Selected In-kind Transfer and Measuring their Impact on Poverty*, US Bureau of Census, Technical Report No. 50 April.

Smeeding, T. (1985) 'Toward better international income estimates: the Luxemburg income study', presented at the IARIW 18th General Conference, Luxemburg, August.

Smolensky, E., W. Pommerehne and R. Dalrymple (1979) 'Postfisc income inequality: a comparison of the United States and West Germany', in J.R. Moroney (ed.), *Income Inequality: Trends and International Comparisons*, Lexington, Mass., Lexington Books.

Stark, T. (1977) *The Distribution of Income in Eight Countries*, Background Paper No. 4, Royal Commission on the Distribution of Wealth, London, HMSO.

Stephenson, G. (1980) 'Taxes, benefits, and the distribution of income', in C.T. Sandford *et al.* (eds), *Taxation and Social Policy*, London, Heinemann, 15–27.

Townsend, P. (1979) *Poverty in the United Kingdom*, Harmondsworth, Penguin.

United Nations (1977) *Provisional Guidelines on Statistics on the Distribution of Income*, Series M, No. 61, New York, United Nations.

Van der Gaag, J. and E. Smolensky (1982) 'Consumer expenditures and the evaluation of levels of living', *Review of Income and Wealth*, 28(1), 17–27.

Van Praag, B., A. Hagenaars and H. van Weeren (1982) 'Poverty in Europe', *Review of Income and Wealth*, 28(4), 345–59.

Wilensky H. (1975) *The Welfare State and Equality*, Berkeley, California, University of California Press.

INDEX

Note References to Canada, Israel, Norway, Sweden, UK, USA and West Germany occur so frequently in the book that they have not been specifically indexed.

Aaron, H., 165
Aberg, R., 55
Achdut, L., ix
  on retirement, 105–25
addresses, 181
administrative data, 13–16
age and income, xviii–xix, 77–104,
  107
  distribution, 85–100
  factor income, 85–7
  fluctuation of economic well-being,
    77–8
  inequality, 91–3
  net income, 87–91, 92–3, 95
  packages, income, 78–85, 96–100,
    101
  and poverty, 77, 93–6, 97, 99–100
  retirement, 66, 103
  single parents, 136
  see also elderly; midlife; young
Aiken, L., 166
Allison, P. D., 104
assistance, social *see* transfers, public
Atkinson, A., ix, xxi, 106
  on income units, 25, 26, 27, 28
  on LIS, xv–xxiii
  on tax-based surveys, 14, 15–17, 19
Australia, 2, 127, 172, 174–7
Austria, 3, 172

Bane, M. J., 160
Bays, K., 166
Beckerman, W., 57
Belgium, 3, 172
benefits *see* transfers, public
Buhmann, B., 55

Canada *see* preliminary note to index
capital, income from *see* property
  income
cash benefits *see* transfers, public
Center for Population, Poverty and
  Policy Studies (CEPS), 2
children
  benefits *see* transfers, public
  care and rearing, 77, 128–9, 135,
    136, 157
  see also families
'cold-deck' imputation, 13, 19
'compressing' income distribution, 49
cost of LIS database, 178–9
counterfactual problem, 23–4
Cowell, F. A., 104
cycle of poverty, 77–8, 93

Danziger, S., 26, 54, 55, 106
database, LIS, 1–19, 172–81
  accessing, 173, 178
  addresses, 181
  cost, 178–9
  definitions, 3–6, 8–11
  demography, 11–12
  development and history, xxi–xxii,
    2–3, 164, 166–7
  equivalent income, 12
  matrices, 174–7
  package, user, 179–80
  quality of data, 12–17
  research and teaching activity,
    180–1
  technical issues of, 3–12
  time series of survey, xx–xxi
  units, 6–8
  user's guide, 172–81

definitions
  equivalence factor/equivalent
    income, 25
  income, 8–11
  issues, 3–6
  retirement, 110–13
demography, 11–12
  and age, 79, 84
  and one-parent families, 130, 131–2
  and poverty, income, 62–5
  and retirement, 107–9
  and social policy research, 162,
    167, 168, 176–7
  see also elderly; midlife; young
Denmark, 126, 172
differentials, wage, 136–7
direct taxes see taxes, direct
disabled, 74, 177
discrimination, sexual, 136
disposable income see net income
distribution and redistribution of
    income, xviii, 20–56
  and age, 85–100
  empirical analysis, 29–51
  equivalence, 38–40, 47–9
  inequality, 33–46
  measure of, 23–4
  methodological issues, 22–9
  one-parent families, 149–56
  rank order, 27–9, 49–51, 52–3
  and retirement, 117–23
  units, 25–9
  see also inequality
dividends from investments see
    property income
double-egalitarian effect, 59

early retirement, 107–23 passim
EARN/BITNET network, 173, 178,
    179
earnings see self-employment; wages;
    zero earnings
economic distance poverty, 62–7
economics, 167, 168–9
Edison, T., xvii
educational qualifications, 136, 176
elderly, 50
  and age differences, 77, 80, 83–95
    passim, 98–104
  database, 4, 16, 18
  and poverty, income, 60–75 passim
  single people, 108–9, 164
  and social policy research, 164,
    165, 166
  see also retirement

Ellwood, D., 160
empirical
  analysis and distribution and
    redistribution of income, 29–51
  results of one-parent families
    research, 131–4
employment
  income from see wages and salaries
  pensions related to see occupational
    pensions
equity and rank order, 49–51, 52–3,
    54
equivalence factor/equivalent income,
    12
  defined, 25
  distribution, 38–40
  net, 89–91, 92–3, 95
  and poverty, income, 58, 75
  and retirement, 118–19, 121–3, 125
  scales, 47–9
  and unit value of income, 25–7
errors, data, 12, 13
Esping-Andersen, G., 161
European Community, 57, 126
European Ministers Responsible for
    Family Affairs, XIIth
    Conference, 126
expenditure, public, 79
  see also transfers

factor income (wages, self-
    employment and property
    income)
  and age, 80–7, 91, 103
  and database, 4, 9–10, 13, 15–17,
    19, 174, 176–7
  and distribution and redistribution
    of income, 23–4, 29–30, 32,
    40–6, 50, 52, 54
  and one-parent families, 126,
    128–9, 131, 134–40, 150, 156–7
  and poverty, income, 66, 68, 73, 74
  and retirement, 110–11, 113–17,
    124
  and social policy research, 164, 168
  see also market income
families (households) generally
  age, 77–91 passim
  and database, xviii, 6–8, 10, 11, 16,
    18
  and distribution and redistribution
    of income, 25–9, 33–6, 40, 42,
    47, 50–1
  and poverty, income, 57–8, 60–5,
    70–5

retirement, 105–25 *passim*
size, 21, 42
   and age, 77, 79, 80, 89
   and one-parent families, 132,
      149–57
   and poverty, 72, 75
   and retirement, 106, 109
   and social policy research, 160, 164
   types of *see* elderly; midlife; one-
      parent families; single; two-
      parent
Fiegehen, G., 6
Finer Report (1974), 126
Finland, 3, 172
First Programme to Combat Poverty,
   EC Commission, 126
Fischer, I., ix
   on one-parent families, 126–57
Ford Foundation, 2, 180
France, 2, 19, 21, 127, 172
Frijs, H., 126
fringe benefits, 165
   see also in-kind

government *see* social policy;
   transfers, public
Greece, 3, 172
gross income
   and age, 80–7, 100, 102, 104
   and database, 9, 175
   and distribution and redistribution
      of income, 20–1, 23–4, 28–50
      passim, 53
   and one-parent families, 146–7
   and poverty, income, 66–71
   and retirement, 113–17, 124

Hauser, R., ix–x
   on income poverty, 57–76
   on one-parent families, 126–57
head of family
   husband as, 79n
   see also women
health care, 162, 165–6, 175
Hedstrom, P., x
   on age and income, 77–104
historical approach, xxi–xxii, 2–3,
   164, 166–7
'horizontal equity', 49
'hot-deck' imputation, 13, 19
households *see* families
housing
   home ownership, 8, 72–3, 75, 177
   rented, 10, 76, 177
   transfers, 165, 166, 175
Hungary, 3, 172

immigrants/aliens, 5, 18, 162
'impact potential', 33
in-kind (non-cash) earnings, 4, 10, 18,
   174, 175
   and social policy research, 164,
      165–6
income
   defined, 8–11
   maintenance *see* transfers
   see also gross income; Luxemburg
      Income Study; net income;
      sources of income
income tax, 18, 104, 124, 149, 168
   and distribution and redistribution
      of income, 31, 32, 50, 54, 174
   see also taxes, direct
individual *see* person; single people
inequality
   and age, 91–3
   comparative, 33–8
   and distribution and redistribution
      of income, 33–46
   and one-parent families, 149–57
   and poverty, 57–62
   sources of, 40–6
insights, policy, 161–3
INSTEAD *see* International Networks
insurance *see* social insurance
international learning process, 22–3,
   159–61
International Networks for Studies of
   Technology, Environment,
   Alternatives and Development,
   2
interstate/interprovincial differences,
   160
investment income *see* property
   income
Ireland, 172
Israel
   excluded from one-parent families
      study, 149
   see also preliminary note to index
Italy, 2, 19, 172

Japan, 21, 172
Jenkins, S., xviii, 54
Johannson, S., 57
Jowell, R., 163

Kahn, A. J., 127, 157
Kamerman, S. B., 127, 157
Kemsley, W., 16
Korpi, W., 58, 161
Kreps, J., 87

labour force participation data, 164,
    168
    see also wages and salaries
Lansley, P., 6
Larsen, O., 163
Lazear, E., 18
learning process, international, 22–3,
    159–61
legislation, 24, 66, 141–2
life cycle concept, 77–8, 93, 167
    see also age
linkages, micro-macro, 164, 168–70
LIS see Luxembourg Income Study
low income see poverty, income
Luxembourg Income Study (LIS),
    xv–xvii
    learning from, xviii–xx
    see also age; database; distribution;
        elderly; families; one-parent;
        poverty; retirement; social
        policy; sources

marginal tax rates, 168
market income (factor income plus
    occupational pensions)
    and age, 80–5, 103
    and database, 4, 9–10, 13, 15–17
    and distribution and redistribution
        of income, 23–4, 29–30, 32,
        43–6
    and one-parent families, 126, 128,
        129, 131, 134–40, 146–8, 150,
        156–7
    and poverty, income, 66, 68, 73, 74
    and retirement, 110–11, 113–17,
        124
matrices of LIS database, 174–7
means-tested benefits see transfers,
    public
medical care, 162, 165–6, 175
methodological issues: distribution
    and redistribution of income,
    22–9
Meyer, J., 165
Michael, R., 18
Micklewright, J., 14, 15, 16, 17, 19
micro-macro linkages, 164, 168–70
midlife families, 57
    and age differences, 79, 82, 86–90,
        92–5, 101–2
    and retirement, 107–23 passim
Millar, J., 132
Mitterrand, F., xx

national accounts, 14–16

negative earnings see zero earnings
net income
    and age, 87–91, 92–3, 95
    and database, 9, 175
    and distribution and redistribution
        of income, 20–1, 23–4, 29, 31,
        34–5, 37–43 passim, 50
    equivalent, 89–91, 92–3, 95
    and one-parent families, 129, 131,
        133, 135, 156
    and poverty, income, 60–72
    and retirement, 106, 114–16,
        118–23, 125
    and social policy research, 165
Netherlands, 2, 126, 172, 174–7
New Zealand, 172
non-cash benefits see in-kind
Norway
    omitted from one-parent families
        survey, 127
    see also preliminary note to index
Nouvertne, U., 57

occupational pensions
    and age, 80–4, 103
    and database, 9–10, 13–14, 15, 16,
        175
    and distribution and redistribution
        of income, 23, 30, 32, 43–5
    and one-parent families, 131
    and poverty, income, 66
    and retirement, 105, 113–16, 124
OECD and publications, xv, 57, 169
    on comparative income distribution,
        163
    inequality comparisons, xvi
    on labour force participation, 138
    on non-cash transfers, 165
    on public expenditure on transfers,
        73, 79, 105, 111
    see also Sawyer
O'Higgins, M., x, xvii
    on comparative social policy
        research, 158–71
    on distribution and redistribution of
        income, 20–56
Oja, G. 15, 54
old people see elderly
one-parent families, xx, xxi, 4,
    126–58
    and database, xx, xxi, 7
    determination of relative economic
        position, 134–49
    distributional aspects, 149–56
    with minor children, 128–34

and poverty, income, 60–4, 66–72, 74
and social policy research, 160, 164
see also under market income: taxes; transfers
Organisation for Economic Cooperation and Development *see* OECD
'original income' *see* pre-transfer income
Orshansky, M., 12

packages
income, and age, 78–85, 96–100, 101
user, for LIS database, 179–80
payroll tax (social insurance), 104, 124, 131, 149, 156, 168
and database, 9–10, 12
and distribution and redistribution of income, 21, 31, 33
see also taxes, direct
pensions *see* occupational pensions; retirement; transfers
per capita income *see* person
person
and distribution and redistribution of income, 27, 28, 35, 40–2, 46–8
equivalent number *see* equivalence
and one-parent families, 133
and poverty, income, 58, 59–62, 66
as unit of analysis, 6–7
see also equivalence; single
Plotnik, R., 49, 56
Poland, 2, 172
policy *see* social policy
pooling of income *see* families
populations *see* demography
post-tax income *see* net income
poverty, income, 57–76
and age, 77, 93–6, 97, 99–100
and database, 5, 6
and demography, 62–5
gaps, 69–72
inequality, 57–62
and one-parent families, 149–57
poverty line, 58–60
rates, 64, 65
and social policy research, 158, 164, 166, 177
transfers and, 60–75
pre-tax income *see* gross income
pre-transfer income, 23
see also market income

private transfers *see* transfers, private
property income
and age, 80–4, 85
and database, 4, 9, 10, 15, 16, 143, 174
and distribution and redistribution of income, 23, 30, 32, 43–5
and one-parent families, 134
and poverty, income, 66
and retirement, 113–17, 124
and social policy research, 164, 168
public expenditure, 79
see also transfers

qualifications, educational, 136, 176
quality of data for LIS database, 12–17

Radner, D., 7, 14, 15, 16, 75, 101–2
Rainwater, L., x, xvi, xvii, 78
on comparative social policy research, 158–71
on income poverty, 57–76
Ramprakash, D., 4, 15, 16
rank order, 36–7
and equity, 49–51, 52–3, 54
and equivalence scales, 47–9
of income units, 27–9, 40
redistribution of income *see* distribution and redistribution of income; transfers, private *and* public
Reeve, S., 163
Rein, M., x, 78
on income poverty, 57–76
relative income, 98
mean, and retirement, 119–21, 124
and one-parent families, 128–34
research, 164–70
retirement, xix, 4, 105–25
age differences *see* elderly; midlife
definitions, 110–13
demography, 107–9
distribution characteristics, 117–23
and social policy research, 159
sources of income 113–17
Ringen, S., x, 55
on age and income, 77–104
Rowntree, S., xviii, 77–8, 91, 93
Ruggles, N. and R., 87
Ruggles, P., 21

salaries *see* wages and salaries
Santer, J., xiv
savings *see* property income

Sawyer, M., on OECD countries, 46,
        54, 163
    France, inequality in, xvi
    per capita distribution, 47
    pre-tax and post-tax concepts, 20–1,
        23, 33, 38
    rankings, 36–7
    see also OECD
scales, equivalence, 47–9
Schaber, G., xi, xvi
    on income poverty, 57–76
Schmaus, G., xi, xiv
    on distribution and redistribution of
        income, 20–56
    on LIS database, 1–19
Schwartz, J., 78, 104
security, social see transfers, public
Selen, J., 55
self-employment
    and age and income, 80–5
    and database, 9, 13, 15, 16, 19, 174
    and distribution and redistribution
        of income, 23, 30, 32, 43–6
    and one-parent families, 134
    and retirement and well-being, 110,
        113–17, 124
    and social policy research, 164
Shamai, N., 157
'shuffling' income distribution, 49
single people
    elderly, 108–9, 124, 164
    parents see one-parent families
    young, 64, 72, 75, 79
    see also person
Smeeding, T. M., xi, xvii, 181
    on comparative social policy
        research, 158–71
    on income poverty, 57–76
    on LIS database, 1–19
Smolensky, E., 12, 21, 106
social change, 167
    see also historical
social insurance
    benefits from see transfers
    payments to see payroll tax
social policy, xiii
    and age, 78, 79, 84
    and distribution and redistribution
        of income, 29, 49
social policy research, comparative,
        significance of LIS for,
        xxi–xxii, 158–71
    income analysis, 163–4
    insights, 161–3

learning about societies, 159–61
    LIS developments and research,
        164–70
social welfare see transfers, public
societies: differences and similarities,
        159–63
sole parents see one-parent families
sources of income see occupational
        pensions; property income;
        self-employment; transfers;
        wages
Spain, 172
standard of living, 25
    relationship with measured income
        see equivalence
    see also poverty, income
Stark, T., 22–3
state see government; transfers, public
Stephenson, G., xi, xiv, 4
    on distribution and redistribution of
        income, 20–56
students, 64, 72, 75, 79
Sutherland, H., xxi
Sweden see preliminary note to index
Switzerland, 2, 172, 174–7

Tamir, Y., xi
    on retirement, 105–25
Taussig, M., 26, 55, 106
tax-based surveys, 14, 15–17, 19
taxes, direct
    and age, 104
    avoidance, 13, 168
    and database, xxi–xxii, 4, 9–10, 12,
        18, 174
    and distribution and redistribution
        of income, 24, 28, 31–3, 37–8,
        40, 47, 49–51, 54
    and one-parent families, 131,
        146–7, 149, 156
    and retirement, 114–17, 124
    and social policy research, 168
    as source of finance see transfers
    tax-based surveys, 13–14
    see also income tax; payroll tax
teaching, 180–1
technical issues of LIS database, 3–12
Tham, H., 55
Thatcher, M., xx
time series of survey, xx–xxi
total money income see gross income
Townsend, P., 57–8
transfers, private (alimony and
        maintenance)

and database, 9
and distribution and redistribution
of income, 23, 31, 54, 175
and one-parent families, 131, 135,
141–3, 146–7, 156, 157
and poverty, income, 61, 66, 68, 74
transfers, public (state benefits and
pensions)
and age, 79–89 passim, 96–100,
104
and database, xxi–xxii, 3–4, 9–10,
11, 15, 17, 18–19
and distribution and redistribution
of income, 23, 31–3, 43–7, 49,
50–1, 54
and one-parent families, 126, 129,
131, 135, 143–8, 150, 156–7
and poverty, income, 60–75
and retirement, 105, 110–17, 124
and social policy research, 164,
165–6, 168
two-parent families
comparison with one-parent
families, 128–33, 135, 137, 142,
146–56
and poverty, income, 60–5, 67,
69–73
and retirement, 108–9

unemployment, 4, 168, 174
and one-parent families, 136
and poverty, 68, 69, 71, 75
United Kingdom see preliminary note
to index
United States see preliminary note to
index
units, income-sharing, 6–8
rank order of, 27–9
value of, 25
weighting of, 26–7
see also families

Van der Gaag, J., 12, 106
Van Praag, B., 12

wages and salaries
and age, 80–5, 103
and database, 4, 9, 10–11, 15–16,
174, 175–6
and distribution and redistribution
of income, 23, 29–30, 32, 43–5
lack of see zero earnings
and one-parent families, 126,
128–9, 134–40, 150, 156–7
and poverty, income, 66, 68, 73, 74
and retirement and well-being, 110,
111, 113–17, 124
and social policy research, 164
wealth
home ownership, 8, 72–3, 75, 177
not taken into account, 75, 157
owner-occupied housing, 177
see also property income
weighting of income–sharing units,
26–7
welfare state
hypotheses about, 161
see also transfers, public
well-being, 49
see also income
West Germany see preliminary note
to index
Wilensky, H., 161
Winship, C., 104
Wolff, E., 54
women as family heads and working,
72, 78, 168
and one-parent families, 136–7

young families, 6–7, 77–95 passim,
101–2, 104, 164
young single people 64, 72, 75, 79

zero earnings, 11, 110–11, 125